Old China

THROUGH THE EYES
OF A STORYTELLER

10/26/23

(sep-87)

To Roberta —
what a pleasure.
meeting you and discovering
so many serendipitous
experiences between us —
Thanks again for
your support of my
Service League program —
Enjoy The journey
to ever —
Judith
Heineman

权衡利弊
奸诈求贤若渴
求贤若渴
假扮礼物
因果循环
谨慎措词
智者
聪慧
七夕
挚爱忠贞
尘缘
奉献

Old China

THROUGH THE EYES
OF A STORYTELLER

AN ANTHOLOGY OF
CHINESE FOLKTALES
AND THE STORIES
BEHIND THEM

Julie Moss Herrera

Parkhurst Brothers, Inc., Publishers

Little Rock

www.parkhurstbrothers.com

Parkhurst Brothers books are distributed to the trade through the Chicago Distribution Center, and may be ordered through Ingram Book Company, Baker & Taylor, Follett Library Resources and other book industry wholesalers. To order from Chicago Distribution Center, phone 1-800-621-2736 or send a fax to 800-621-8476. Copies of this and other Parkhurst Brothers Inc., Publishers titles are available to organizations and corporations for purchase in quantity by contacting Special Sales Department at our home office location, listed on our web site. Manuscript submission guidelines for this publishing company are available at our web site.

Printed in the United States of America

First Edition, 2012

2012 2013 2014 2015 2016 2017   12 11 10 9 8 7 6 5 4 3 2 1

Library of Congress Cataloging-in-Publication Data

Herrera, Julie Moss, 1947-
 Old China through the eyes of a storyteller : an anthology of Chinese folktales and the stories behind them / Julie Moss Herrera.
     p. cm.
 Includes bibliographical references and index.
 ISBN 978-1-935166-85-6 (alk. paper) -- ISBN 1-935166-85-9 (alk. paper) -- ISBN 978-1-935166-86-3 -- ISBN 1-935166-86-7
 1. Tales--China. 2. Oral tradition--China. 3. Storytelling--China. I. Title.
 GR335.H64 2012
 398.20951--dc23

                              2012012511

 ISBN: Original Trade Paperback   978-1-935166-85-6   [10 digit: 1-935166-85-9]
 ISBN: e-book   978-1-935166-86-3   [10-digit: 1-935166-86-7]

This book is printed on archival-quality paper that meets requirements of the American National Standard for Information Sciences, Permanence of Paper, Printed Library Materials, ANSI Z39.48-1984.

Cover and page design:	Harvill-Ross Studios Ltd.
Acquired for Parkhurst Brothers Inc., Publishers	
And edited by:	Ted Parkhurst
Proofreader:	Barbara Paddack

112012

Dedicated to my daughter,
Laura Metz,
who gave me the courage to travel to China,
and my son,
Phillip Metz
who taught me how to market the stories.

Acknowledgements

This book would not have been possible without the assistance of many people. Laura Metz, my daughter, gave me the courage to travel to China and then accompanied me on the trip. Phil Metz, my son, guided me through the marketing process and encourged me to brag more. My Chinese friends, interpreters, and story lovers: Huáng Kānglè Sky, for his gifts of stories and guidance with the story content, Li Kuo, for his work in preparing the pinyin used in the Pinyin Glossary, Yan Lixian, for her unflagging enthusiasm and delight in our group, Zhang Xiaosong, for her exuberant discussions on a long bus ride, Zhang Xiaoping, for listening to the early versions of some of the stories. Rafe Martin and his workshop Writing for Storytellers; Cathryn Fairlee shared her Masters' Thesisan and became a friend and along with Joel Ben Izzy both of whom I met at the July, 2010, NSN Conference helped me believe I could complete the book project. Barbara Kolupke read and edited early drafts and offered helpful insight. I owe a great debt to Judith Henieman for oh so many details, discussions, friendship and for allowing me to use her adaptation of Across the Bridge Rice Noodles. Taos Storytellers, students in Sheila Sanchez's class and all the others who listened to and helped me refine the stories deserve my great thanks. I will forever remember the Chinese people for gifting stories to me and others in our group. Nancy Wang and Robert Kikuchi-Yngojo, better known as Eth-no-tec, generously traded travel stories with me. My friend, Jack Rudder, provided the Civil War story Huáng Kānglè Sky had been searching for. The National Storytelling Network and People to People Ambassador Program graciously and professionally provided the opportunity to travel half way 'round the world to unearth and collect these stories.

For navigation guidance in the publishing business a big thank you goes to Ted Parkhurst of Parkhurst Brothers Publishing for taking a chance on an unknown storyteller/writer as well as for his guidance and editing. I would like to acknowledge Rick Frishman and Robyn Freedman Spizman and their book series Author 101. For the beautiful cover design and book illustrations I have Charlie Ross to thank.

A big thank you goes out to all my friends and family, far and near, who cheered me on, especially Lila Henry, the Survivors fellow retired educators, and Donna Wehe. To storytellers Cherie Karo Schwartz, Don "Buck" Creacy and Mike Lockett for their support and to our intrepid Chinese Tour group of ten brave souls who embarked upon a life-changing journey together not knowing where it would end my heartfelt thanks.

Finally my husband, Geno Herrera, has earned stars in his eternal crown for graciously accepting my harried schedules, far-away dreams, crazy ideas and long stretches at the computer. Thank you, Geno.

– J.M.H.

Table of Contents

Introduction

Huáng Kānglè Sky

Three years ago, Julie visited China as a delegate with the storytelling delegation from the American People to People Ambassador Program. I have been a story lover since I was a kid, so I was very happy to meet all the delegates. I remembered an American story I heard once which is called A Horseman in the Sky, and that my tears could not help falling as I listened to the story with great attention. I asked Julie for more information about this story; Julie kindly emailed me with the story and information concerning the American Civil War. Julie helped me, a Chinese story lover, obtain an in depth understanding of American stories.

Then it was Julie's turn to have a great interest in our Chinese culture, she had gained much firsthand access to Chinese stories during her visit to China. And she mentioned her intention of writing an anthology of Chinese stories. I was so happy and surprised to hear that, but also boggled: those ancient Chinese stories are so far away from America by many years and even more miles, how can they speak to American readers? Julie kept searching and studying for Chinese stories through every possible means. Her love of Chinese stories drove her to put all her heart and persistence into carrying on. Two years passed, she finished writing this book; I found out it is a great surprise. The pictures of those stories I knew as a child came alive again in my mind as I was reading them from the perception of Julie's mind. Every detail from my imagination coincides with Julie's reorganization. I suddenly realized how much effort she had made during the past two years.

For this anthology Julie picked stories from a great variety of old Chinese stories, such as the fable story The Snipe and the Mussel (Clam) from the Strategies of Warring States Period of China, the folktale of the White Snake, the constellation story of Weaving Fair Lady and Water Buffalo Boy and others. It is a wonderful choice of stories and a vivid reorganization. Every story is followed with an author's note and considerate storytelling tips. It is a very good book for beginner readers of Chinese stories and also would be a useful tool for storytellers as well.

I enjoyed reading the book a lot. When I was in the mood for reading something I would open the manuscript and make myself a cup of tea, then I could totally relax myself and find the pure delight in reading. It's a magical book offered to readers with access to profound Chinese culture. I would recommend it to all of my friends and story lovers. We may spend some time finding the childhood leisure of listening to or reading a story book to escape from a fussy world.

– H. K. S.

Preface

In the world of storytelling, discovering a story you are meant to tell can be as easy as it is poignant or as difficult as it is pleasurable. Some stories scream "TELL ME! TELL ME!" Others whisper softly, "I am the one you want." And once in awhile you stumble across a story you know in your heart was meant just for you. Every storyteller has his/her favorite way of finding stories. Mine was to read anthologies, picking and choosing stories which sang to my heart.

But having the opportunity to travel half a world away to collect stories never occurred to me until the letter came. Then another one. I wanted to discuss going to China with my daughter, but she was literally out to sea. So we started an email conversation. She urged me to live on the edge and go, taking her with me. I felt safer. You see, she is the only person I knew at that time who had traveled to China and lived to tell about the many wonders she had seen.

So I answered the letters at the last possible moment and was accepted as a Storytelling Delegate for the National Storytelling Network and People to People Ambassadors' Storytelling Tour of China. That was in September; we would leave in April. I had six months to prepare. I learned The Young Head of the Household and told it whenever I talked to children about my trip to China. For this story I needed some props, which became part of my list of souvenirs to purchase in China. I enlisted the help of my church with donations of gifts for the children we would meet in a rural area of China. I selected photos I had taken of the farming area in Colorado where I live to take as gifts for our guides and those who would honor us with engagements, gatherings and conferences.

I bought journals in which to record the stories to be

heard. I made lists and revised them weekly. I read about the history of Old China and the turmoil of the 20th century. Two autobiographies which helped me understand not only Old China but modern China as well were *Falling Leaves* by Adeline Yen Mah and *Wild Swans* by Jung Chang. The public library was a rich resource for children's books full of wonderful pictures of the places we would visit. I read folktales in picture books, anthologies and on the internet. And when my daughter came home she helped me select my travel wardrobe. By April I thought I was ready to travel half way 'round the world to unearth stories worth bringing back to share with my home audiences.

Our adventure actually started in San Francisco's China Town, where my cousin introduced my daughter and me to the sights and sounds of China away from China. As my cousin, daughter and I toured China Town, we heard Chinese being spoken on the street and in the shops wherever we ventured. The aroma of spices, herbs and other unfamiliar scents rose up to engulf us. We savored the foods. Next, on to the airport to meet the rest of our group of fourteen intrepid travelers. Then off we flew across the Pacific, through the night and into the next day of Asian mystery.

Beijing is an enormous city of approximately 15 million people spread out over 17,000 square kilometers. Although we were warned not to venture too far afield on our own, and none of us did except my daughter who knew where she was going and what to do, we felt safe in our little neighborhood surrounding the hotel where we stayed. Our national guide, Yan Lixian, was a wonderfully warm and friendly woman who took us all under her wing, making us feel welcome and special by teaching us a few important phrases in Mandarin, putting us in taxis with special instructions to the drivers, and spending time speaking with each of us individually. We were ferried quickly and gently through the traffic by our marvelous bus drivers. Liang Liang, our Beijing guide further enhanced our knowledge of the people and cultures of China. He gave us the nickname "Sticky Rice" when we visited Tia'anmen Square because as storytellers we were all prone to wander off in order to see something that interested us.

In Beijing, several stories claimed me. There was the Tale of Lady White or The White Snake which I heard a bit of during our meeting with the China Folklore Society in the library of a Daoist Temple where we all sat around a red oval table in red chairs the afternoon of our first day. Dr. Kang Li, who had done much research on this story, speaking through our interpreter told us only the ending about Lady White's son finding her and setting things aright. Following the discussion about folktales, she gave each of us a copy of one of her folktale books. Mine was about Lady White. Although I could not read it because it is, of course, written in Chinese, there are pictures. I was intrigued with the concept of the life force, Qì, which could enable a spirit animal to take on another form after one thousand years. Another story from the members of the China Folklore Society was an abbreviated version of Tears that Crumbled the Great Wall also known as Lady Meng Jiang Wailed at the Great Wall, a story of love and devotion. Dr. Yang Lihui, China's first PhD in folklore, told us the story of The Snipe and the Mussel, which she explained as a fable told by one king to another to promote a peaceful end to war. As we sat at long folding tables near the entrance of the Jiu Xian Qiao Community Center, Mr. Wong told us Longevity. The Center, established for retired electrical workers, plays an important role in their lives by giving the retired workers a place to gather, learn and share. Mr. Wong is one of the calligraphy teachers at the Center. The Chinese still revere the wisdom of the elders. An elder's place in society is that of a Wise Guide. I related to the philosophy at the heart of Beijing's establishment of centers for retirees as this is the basis of Spellbinders, a volunteer storytelling group to which I belong.

From Beijing we traveled southwest to the mountain city of Guiyang where we met Huáng Kānglè (Sky), our Guizhou Province guide. Yan Lixian told us Butterfly Lovers while we rested under the roof of an open pagoda in a beautiful setting on our way up to see the Dragon's Gate Cave. This beautifully haunting tale, reminiscent of Shakespeare's Romeo and Juliet, is a much older tale than its British counterpart. Huáng Kānglè Sky, a true story lover, entertained us on our long bus rides from place to place with many short stories. Among them, Huáng Kānglè Sky told It Is Worth a Thousand Li Feather, which illustrates such dedication to a task that I thought it perfect to tell young children who have trouble accomplishing difficult assignments. Weaving Fair Lady and Buffalo Boy also called The Magpie Bridge is not only a love story, but also a star story. Star stories are some of my favorite folktales. My father, an amateur astrologer, used to tell my sisters and me short versions of the stories about constellations as we gazed up at the night sky. I can still find a number of the constellations and tell a few of the stories. A version of The Thousand Li Horse was also among the stories Huáng Kānglè Sky told us, which indicates it is wise to find a way to increase your return on an investment.

In Shanghai we were entertained by school children who were in fifth or sixth grade. One group of boys put on the play Tuiqiao – Push or Knock – complete with costumes, but no donkey. This complicated drama about writing is another story especially suited to children who are learning to write. It shows they are not the only ones who have difficulty choosing the best words.

I would have liked more stories to claim me, but it was time to leave. One final story found its way to me only after my return to the United States. Because Huáng Kānglè Sky was so interested in American history, he had asked me to send him a Civil War legend about a man and his son who were on opposing sides. Upon my return home, I asked my friend Jack, who is a Civil War re-enactor. He did know the story which turned out to be "A Horseman in the Sky", in which a young southerner who has joined the Union Army must decide whether or not to shoot his own father. Jack told me the story and gave me a book with a version of the legend. I combined Jack's version and the one in the book, and sent the result to Huáng Kānglè Sky. He rewarded me with The Tiger, a universal story about bravery in the face of extreme danger; and who among us has not at least imagined facing that situation?

Back home in Colorado, I realized I needed a few more stories to round out this anthology. Where would I find them? I began my search in the small anthology I had purchased when researching some of the fables I was already telling. Here I found a version of The Man Who Pretended He Could Play Reed Pipes. I thought it interesting that even so long ago in Ancient China there were people pretending to be what they were not. We see that so often today; so why not include this story. When I told an old friend about writing a book of Chinese Folktales, he asked, "Are you going to include this one?" while he proceeded to tell a version of A Blessing or a Curse? I already knew of that story and so into the mix it went.

Because I had heard my friend and fellow traveler, Judith Heineman tell Across the Bridge Rice Noodles which she learned from our wonderful Chinese guide Yan Lixian, I asked for and was granted permission to include it as the only story I do not tell myself. This is another story of love and devotion where through love and kindness a man and woman are drawn closer together their lives enriched by a warm lunch .

In looking at the love stories included in this anthology, I found that in most of them the element of arranged marriage was missing for the two who were in love. I wonder, perhaps that was the appeal to the Chinese who for so long had their marriages arranged for them by parents, relatives and match-makers. I don't know for sure, but to the western mind it makes sense.

And so my journey seems complete, and yet I am reluctant to stop my travels, both physical and mental into the area of Chinese storytelling and stories. To say my trip half way 'round the world was life changing is an understatement. It has forever changed my view of the Chinese people, I have a better understanding of Chinese beliefs, and I know I have only touched the tip of the iceberg here in this book. Will I ever return to China? There is a good possibility that I might. But that's another story for another time.

– J.M.H.

权衡利弊

The Snipe and the Mussel (Clam)

A Fable from China
(475-221 BC)

Retold by Dr. Yang Lihui
Professor of Folklore and Anthropology at
Beijing Normal University
Director of the China Folklore Society

As a Clam was basking in the sun, a Snipe happened along. The Snipe thought, "Yummm! Lunch!" Walking carefully on its long legs, the Snipe sneaked up behind the Clam and started to peck at it. Immediately the Clam shut its shell, grabbing the Snipe's long beak and refusing to let go. So they tugged and they pulled, and they pulled and they tugged; but neither could get loose.

Through its nose, the Snipe exclaimed, "If it doesn't rain today or tomorrow, you will die here on the beach!"

"If you can't get yourself loose today or tomorrow, there will be a dead Snipe on the beach too!" retorted the Clam through its clenched shell.

Neither of them would let go.

That evening when a fisherman happened by, he thought

"Yummmm! Dinner!" and caught them both. Laughing, the fisherman said, "You are both bulls!" meaning they were both too stubborn for their own good. Then he took them home and made clam and snipe stew.

Author's Notes

During the Warring States Period, this tale was used by one king to suggest to another king that they should no longer fight each other because neither was winning and both were losing. It also shows that, when both are losing a fight someone stronger will be able to defeat both adversaries. Today The Snipe and the Mussel is considered a peace story. (Yang)

I did tell this story to my senator and former representative in 2010. Perhaps it needed a retelling during the summer of 2011.

Storytelling Tips

The Snipe and the Mussel is the first story I learned to tell upon my return from China. It was easy to learn because it is so short, but there is a powerful message in this story, one that is needed as much today as it was 2300 years ago.

This is such a fun story to tell! It works especially well in classrooms where the need for compromise is great. After the story, children enjoy a short discussion on how to save face and get themselves out of a potentially dangerous situation.

When telling the story, I pinch my nose to sound like the snipe and speak through clenched teeth when the clam is talking.

The Tiger
or
Fox Assumes Tiger's Authority

Traditional Chinese story which is over 2300 years old

Retold by Huáng Kānglè Sky
Tour Guide and Translator in Guizhou Province

Once, there was a very powerful Tiger living deep in the forest who wished to eat one hundred different animals, proving to himself that he really was King of the Forest as the mark on his forehead indicated. So he set such goal for himself. Since he was a very powerful animal his wish gradually came true.

The day Tiger was in search of his 100th animal of prey, Fox crossed Tiger's path. Tiger stretched out his large paw and heavily placed it upon Fox's tail. When Tiger opened his mouth wide to swallow him, Fox suddenly spoke, "Do you think you will be the King of the Forest after eating me?"

"No you will not," said Fox answering his own question. "Tiger, you dare not eat me for I am the King of the Forest proclaimed by the Heavenly Emperor. If you eat me, you will be punished with death by the Heavenly Emperor. Whoever eats me will meet this fate!"

Tiger half believed Fox's tale. He thought, "Every animal

in the forest when caught by my terrible claws is in a great panic and scared to death. Only with the Heavenly Emperor's blessing can Fox be so calm and arrogant." But to Fox he said, "Prove it!"

Fox spoke, "Tiger, are you doubting the truth? Come and follow me into the forest I will prove it to you!"

Fox walked into the forest with Tiger following closely behind. Soon, they got to the deepest part of the forest where many animals lived. Hare saw Fox followed by ... Tiger, and ran away to warn the others. Deer and Gazelle looked up and saw Fox followed by ... Tiger. At the same time they heard Hare's warning, both bounded off deeper into the forest. Monkey saw Fox followed by ... Tiger from the trees and climbed higher so as to be out of reach. Cobra slithered away as fast as he could when he saw Fox followed by ... Tiger. Even Elephant ran when he saw Fox followed by ... Tiger.

Then Fox turned his head around, looked at Tiger and said, "See? All the animals ran away because they saw me coming. I am the fiercest animal in the world by the proclamation of the Heavenly Emperor! You cannot eat me!"

Tiger was taken in by Fox's sly trick, and ran back out of the forest as fast as he could without looking behind him even once.

How was Fox successfully able to trick Tiger? Tiger did not realize all the animals were actually scared away by his appearance behind Fox.

Author's Notes

Long, long ago in the Warring States Period of Ancient China, there was an independent state called Chu in the middle part of China. The Lord Xuan of Chu (362 BCE) was very confused by why all the states in the north were afraid of his general, Zhao Xixu, but not of him. Therefore he summoned his chancellery for an answer.

A smart minister named Jiang Yi told a story to Lord Xuan. Fox Assumes Tiger's Authority is the story that Jiang Yi told, suggesting that the northern states were not afraid of General Zhao Xixu but of his overwhelming army just as all the animals were actually scared away by Tiger's appearance behind Fox. This was a face saving way of telling the Lord Xuan that he was really the most powerful without hurting the feelings of the general. The state of Chu was largest and most southern of the Warring States. (Huang)

This story of tiger originates from the Zhan Guo Se (Strategies of the Warring States), which is a renowned ancient Chinese compilation of intermittently written materials about the Warring States Period. This historical work was actually compiled between the 3rd to 1st centuries BCE about two hundred years after the Warring States had been subdued. It is an important text of the Warring States Period as it reports the strategies and political views of the School of Negotiation and reveals the historical and social characteristics of the period. (Cultural China) Strategies of the Warring States consists of 33 scrolls recording the fables and stories of the twelve different Warring States of Ancient China. The story called Fox Assumes Tiger's Authority comes from the first scroll of the state of Chu, a state located in the middle of today's China. (Huang)

Tigers really are known "as the King of the Forest in China because markings on their heads resemble the Chinese character for King." (Chai)

Storytelling Notes

The story of the Tiger and the Fox is so enjoyable to tell because of Fox's attitude. He can be as arrogant as the teller can make him! After telling this story to a group of fifth graders who were learning stories of their own to tell, one boy asked if he could tell "The Fox Assumes Tiger's Authority." Hearing, "Yes," he told the story with such gusto; the fox really had quite an attitude problem. But then the Tiger burst out, "Prove it!" So with his permission now that is part of my telling too.

When Fox and Tiger are conversing, Fox always looks up at Tiger and Tiger looks down his nose at Fox. "Fox followed by … (gasp and terrified look) Tiger" can become an audience participation element of the story. Doing this indicates just how scared the animals all are of Tiger, not Fox.

If the audience is preschoolers or kindergartners, after telling the story instead of the question written above, I usually ask, "Why did all the animals run away from Fox?" And am told, "It wasn't Fox who scared the animals, it was Tiger!" Surprising at what a young age they know. This is my young grandson's favorite story which he simply calls The Tiger.

Fox Assumes Tiger's Authority is a great story to preface a discussion on bullying, because it can be used to show what happens when the person who is being bullied turns the tables upon the one doing the bullying. Here is a more peaceful ending to the conflict than anyone being eaten or beaten.

求贤若渴 求贤若渴

The Thousand Li Horse
or
Buying a Good Horse

Retold by Huáng Kānglè Sky
Tour Guide and Translator in Guizhou Province

A king wanted a good horse that could travel one thousand li (Chinese mile) without stopping. Did such a horse exist? He sent out a proclamation: "The King is offering to pay one thousand pieces of gold for a horse that can travel one thousand li."

After a while a man, who worked for the king, came forward saying, "I shall find such a horse and shall take it to the king myself."

So the king gave the man one thousand pieces of gold to pay for the horse when he found it. The man traveled far and asked everyone he met if they knew of such a horse. No one did until at last an old farmer said, "I have just the horse for you, but you must let me help you bring it to the king."

"Very well," said the man. "Show me the horse."

The old farmer led the man to his tumble down barn. There in the far corner was an ancient horse, more dead than alive. "I shall ride my horse to the king and accept the gold from his hand," declared the old farmer.

"Wait a minute," replied the man. "That old horse won't

make it to the next town."

"Then you won't have to pay full price," bargained the farmer.

The man and the farmer rode off headed for the king's residence. Indeed the farmer's horse died in route to the next town. "See," pointed out the man, "that horse did not make it to the next town."

"Indeed not," returned the old farmer. "Therefore you only owe me five hundred pieces of gold."

"What?" shouted the man. "Five hundred pieces of gold for this dead horse? Ridiculous!"

"No, no!" exclaimed the old farmer. "Let me explain to you why you must pay the five hundred pieces of gold for my poor old horse."

And with that he began to whisper in the man's ear. The man nodded from time to time, and the upshot was that the man took only the horse's skull to the king, arriving three months later than he should have.

The king was relieved to hear his horse had been delivered. But when he saw only the horse's skull and the man told what he had paid for it, the king was enraged. "This horse cannot travel anywhere!" he roared. "I want a live horse! Five hundred pieces of gold for a horse's skull? You should not have paid anything for the skull of a horse that died while trying to travel a thousand li."

"Wait!" the man cried bowing low. "Most Honorable King, I told the old farmer the same thing, but he explained it all to me as I will now explain it to you."

"What?" retorted the king. "You are crazy. Take him away!"

"No, no," pleaded the man. "Your majesty, please listen. If you are willing to pay five hundred pieces of gold for a horse's skull, won't you give more for a live horse? The old farmer is already happily telling people about your generosity. I shall also tell everyone I meet how generous you are. Then you will see how many fine horses will quickly come your way!"

Reluctantly the king agreed the price of five hundred pieces of gold was fair if he received some good news soon. The man left and did tell everyone he met of the king's generosity. Soon the king had many fine horses to choose from. He purchased the three that pleased him the most.

Author's Notes

In Ancient China a perfect horse was known as a thousand li horse (qian li ma). This horse was said to be able to run a thousand li without rest. We might call the horse a world class horse. Horses were believed to be of utmost value and during the later dynasties a quality horse could be traded for forty bolts of Chinese silk. Qian li ma were also known as tianma or heavenly horses. (Michaelson)

A li is a Chinese unit of measurement, usually translated as "mile." However a Chinese li is not the same distance as an American mile. According to the Chinese Measurement Converter (http://www.mandarintools.com/measures.html), 1 kilometer = 2 li = 0.621 miles. (Peterson) May Lee Chai, in China A-Z, says "A li equals one third mile." So, 1000 li is approximately 310-333 American miles.

A Thousand Li Horse is another fable from the Warring States Period (475-221 BCE) which was told to Prince Zhao of Yan by Master Guo Wei at a time when the king was trying to rebuild his kingdom. Huáng Kānglè (Sky) explained to us that when the king agreed to purchase the skull of the dead horse at half the original price for a live horse, he showed that he knew five hundred pieces of gold for a skull would gather many fine horses for him or really many fine advisors.

There is a later version of the story which comes from

the Three Kingdoms Period (220-280 CE). During this period of Ancient Chinese history the emperors of the three states of Wei, Shu and Wu all claimed the right of descent from the Han Dynasty. Theirs was another time of bloody feuding which has been romanticized by modern tellers and writers. One of the serialized stories now told in the Yangzhou teahouses is about the Romance of the Three Kingdoms, which greatly romanticizes the Three Kingdoms Period. But here is the short story of A Thousand Li Horse.

A Thousand Li Horse
(Version from 220-280 CE)

A man, known as Bole whose real name was Sun Yang, was the best person to judge a horse. When it was pointed out to him by a high official of the court, Duke Mu of Qin, that he was growing no younger and needed to find a successor, Bole replied, "None of my children are worthy of my position, but I know of a laborer who is just as good as I."

The laborer, Jiufang Gao, was hired and sent out to find a Thousand Li Horse for the king. After three months he sent word saying he had found just the horse. When pressed for a description he sighed, "A yellow mare."

But the horse was a black stallion. When the official who had hired the laborer heard the horse was a black stallion instead of a yellow mare, he was infuriated. But Bole told him, "Jiufang Gao has now exceeded even his own ability! A judge of horses sees only the nature of the horse, not peripheral features."

When the horse arrived it was the most magnificent black stallion – a thousand li horse just as had been promised. The official was pleased, as was the king.

Bole's lesson: "Forgetting what is coarse, he obtains the essence. ... He sees what he sees and forgets what he does not see." (Schrist)

Another interpretation of the stories comes much later from Han Yu, a great Tang Dynasty (618-907 CE) poet, scholar and official. Han Yu's interpretation explains that the stories are not really about horses and whether they are gifted runners, but about the need of a ruler to attract and cultivate gifted advisors. (Schrist)

Storytelling Tips

In telling this story, I usually tell first the story I heard in China and then the later version which I found in my own research. This helps the audiences of upper elementary students on up see how a story might travel not only over a distance to another part of the country or even another culture but also through time to another much later period when again it is needed to make a point. A short commentary about the Warring States Period and the Three Kingdoms Period also helps the audience see the similarities in these two periods in Chinese history.

In the Warring States version there are some fun voices to play with – the old farmer, the petulant king and the man who is the seeker and plays two roles, that of an underling and that of one who must get his business right. The characters posture and gestures can also give hints into their personalities.

The Three Kingdoms version has similar varied characters which can be given various voices, postures and gestures.

假扮

The Man Who Pretended He Could Play the Reed Pipes

Adapted from Ancient Chinese Fables and other sources
Attributed to the philosopher, Han Fei Tzu

"Làn yú chōng shù" or "to fill a position without having the necessary qualifications" is the dramatic situation in this old Chinese story.

King Xuan of Qi loved hearing the music of the yú, a melodious open reed pipe, so much that he formed the royal court orchestra comprised only of yú players. The men playing in the orchestra drew a good salary, many more times that of a street merchant. Although they were always on call to the king, the musicians and their families lived in comfort.

There was one scholarly man who coveted the salary of the orchestra players although he, himself, could not play a note. His name was Nanguo. "Oh, that I could make money so easily," he thought.

So he set off for the palace purchasing a yú along the way. When the merchant who sold the yú to Nanguo asked, "Would you like me to show you how to play?" Nanguo only answered gruffly, "No!"

At the palace bowing low, he asked, "May I have an audience with the king?"

"State your business here!" demanded the guards.

"I have come seeking a place in the royal orchestra," Nanguo answered politely.

The guards conferred with one another, then one came forward, "The king is in need of one more yú player. Follow me."

Nanguo followed the guard through the palace until they reached the throne of King Xuan. Bowing low, the guard stated, "Oh honorable king, this humble man has come seeking a place in your royal orchestra and wishes to speak with you."

The king looked Nanguo over while he stood with his head bowed. Then he invited, "Come closer and tell me about yourself."

Nanguo was overjoyed but tried very hard not to show it. He slowly walked forward keeping his head down; then bowing low began, "Honorable King, I have heard that you are seeking one more yú player for your great orchestra. I believe I am the man you are seeking as I am one of the finest players in the region where I come from."

They conversed for a while longer with the king not once asking Nanguo to play the yú for him. The king was so taken by Nanguo that he offered him twice the salary of the other musicians. And, of course, Nanguo politely accepted, all the while grinning to himself.

Nanguo smiled contentedly. "Now my life is easy," he said to himself when he went shopping for new clothes.

"Now I can eat well," he said as he went shopping for great quantities of food.

And even though he was surrounded by masters, Nanguo never even bothered to learn anything more than how to sit in the back row and pretend to play, never ever blowing a single note. The orchestra sounded wonderful without his playing; so he continued to pretend.

Eventually King Xuan died and was replaced by his son, Prince Min. Now Prince Min also loved hearing the beautiful melodies from the yú. But instead of a whole orchestra, he preferred to hear one pipe at a time. Since there were so many players, enough for a different one to play each day of the year, he summoned a different yú player each day.

Nanguo never volunteered to be the one to play for Prince Min but stayed on at the palace drawing his large salary until the last day of the year when it would be his turn to play a solo performance on his yú. The night before he was to be called into Prince Min's court, he ran away. So when the guards came looking for him, he was nowhere to be found.

Author's Notes

While working on some of the other stories, I happened across a small volume entitled, Ancient Chinese Fables, containing sixty-three fables, which--according to the preface--"have stood the test of time." Some of the fables we had heard in China, but others we had not. One fable from Ancient Chinese Fables struck me as being quite interesting and appropriate for our times since it speaks to doing that for which we neither have been trained nor have a talent. That short two paragraph fable had a title almost as long as the fable itself: The Man Who Pretended He Could Play Reed Pipes.

So, with further research, I expanded the story and added dialogue to make it more interesting and then told the story to a group of my daughter's musician friends. They loved it. Now it is a standard of my Chinese repertoire.

Han Fei Tzu was a prince of the House of Han, who put his energies into writing since he was not an eloquent speaker and actually stuttered. He believed that humans by nature are deceitful and need moral guidance. Thus he cautioned rulers should richly reward their ministers who were loyal and faithfully carried out their duties, but harshly punish those who were disloyal or dishonest and deceitful. (Knoblock) Han Fei Tzu's philosophy may explain why Nanguo hightailed it out of the court when it was his turn to play the yú by himself.

Storytelling Tips

I found a picture of the yú which I display at performances so listeners can see what the ancient Chinese reed pipe looks like.

Nanguo can be a pompous know-it-all who is a bit lazy. Yet he knows when it is in his best interest to speak politely in order to get his way. Because of his dual personae, Nanguo's voice changes from when he speaks as a know-it-all to a man interviewing for a position in the royal orchestra.

礼物

It Is Worth a Thousand Li Feather

The story behind a Famous Chinese Proverb
Retold by Huáng Kānglè (Sky)
Tour Guide and Translator in Guizhou Province

The officer said to his soldier, "We have one important task to do. We must take this goose to the Emperor to break his Holy Fast."

So the soldier carried the goose as both he and his officer started on their journey. The Emperor's palace was 1000 li (Chinese miles) away. They walked and they walked and they walked, traveling many li before the soldier was so tired he could go no further. He said to his officer, "I need to rest."

"So do I," said the officer. So they put the goose down on the ground and tied a string loosely to one of its legs with the other end tied loosely around a small tree. Then the men fell asleep.

While the soldier and the officer were sleeping, the goose escaped, leaving behind only one feather. When the soldier awoke, he looked around for the goose but could not find it anywhere. He even looked in the nearby pond. The soldier dutifully woke his superior officer and explained, "I cannot find that silly goose anywhere. I have looked all over and the only thing I found was this one goose feather."

"Hmmm," replied the officer. "I think we should just take the feather to the Emperor instead of looking any further for that run-away goose. Let us go."

They walked on and on for several days and finally reached the Emperor's palace tired and footsore. As they walked, the officer made up a story poem about their adventures which is now known throughout China as this proverb: "Qiān l ǐ sòng é máo ; l ǐ qīng qíng yì zhòng ." Or in English "The gift is very light, but the passion is huge."

Author's Notes

In English, as translated by Victor H. Mair in The Columbia History of Chinese Literature, we would say, "[When] a goose feather is sent a thousand miles, [although] the gift [itself] is light, the [accompanying] sentiment is weighty."

Others have translated it as: "Sending you a goose feather from a thousand miles; the gift is light but the love is strong." ("Tansname.com: Chinese/Kanji Tattoo Design")

"A goose feather sent from thousands of miles away is a present little in size but rich in meaning." (Li and Ding) In our Western culture, we say, "It's the thought that counts."

A li is a Chinese unit of measurement, usually translated as "mile." However a Chinese li is not the same distance as an American mile. According to the Chinese Measurement Converter (http://www.mandarintools.com/measures.html), 1 kilometer = 2 li = 0.621 miles. (Peterson) May Lee Chai, in China A-Z, says "A li equals one third mile." So, 1000 li is approximately 310-333 American miles.

Storytelling Tips

A goose feather makes an appropriate prop for this very short tale. In my version, the soldier is usually demonstrative and uses many gestures when talking about the missing goose to his superior. The officer is more reserved and detached, but alarmed, nonetheless. To indicate how far the soldier and his officer walked, I use Mime walking while I am telling that part of the story. I start out fast and the slow down to indicate their growing exhaustion. This part of the story can be expanded to include as many days as the teller wishes. Audience members may be encouraged to mime walk as well.

因果循环

A Blessing or a Curse?

Also known as
The Lost Horse or Bad Luck, Good Luck

Adapted from a survey of anthologies,
a picture book and additional research.

Old Sai was very good at interpreting events and was known throughout his village on the northern border as a wise man.

One day Old Sai's only horse, a strong, fast mare, ran off. His neighbors visited him in small groups saying, "What bad luck that your horse ran away." "It is a curse to lose a fine horse such as yours."

But Old Sai merely shook his head and replied, "And what makes you think this is a curse? All may turn out well yet."

Several weeks later the mare returned with a strong, fast stallion from the northern border tribes. Again his neighbors came to Old Sai, saying, "This is good luck! Your horse came back and now you have a fine strong stallion as well! Blessings have surely come your way."

Old Sai shook his head and laughed, "A blessing? Perhaps not. Things are rarely what they seem"

Later that year Old Sai's son was riding the new stallion; he fell from the saddle and broke his leg. The villagers returned to

Old Sai's home lamenting his ill fortune. "Ahh, and now your son has broken his leg, what bad luck. There must be a curse on that stallion."

Old Sai shook his head once more, "Bad luck, a curse, you say? This may not be so bad after all."

The next year the Tribes from the North invaded China and all able bodied men were asked to take up arms and fight. When the bloody battles were over, nine out of ten of the men who had gone to fight lost their lives. Because Old Sai's son was lame from his fall, he could not go and so was his life saved. Old Sai and his son were able to care for each other for many more years.

When his neighbors tried to congratulate him once again, Old Sai wisely said, "Change is inevitable. A blessing can become a curse; and a curse can be a blessing in disguise. It is an unfathomable mystery."

Author's Notes

An old friend, when he heard I was writing this anthology, told me the story about the Lost Horse and asked if I were including it. Originally I had not planned to include it, but when asked to flesh out the manuscript, it was one of the first stories I thought of including. The title here, A Blessing or a Curse? is how I knew the story.

Since Sai Weng or Old Sai is the name of the wise villager in many of the versions I found, I decided to use his name. Then I found the following explanation of the story written by J. Lau: "Sai Weng Shi Ma … is actually a commonly used Chinese idiom or chengyu. It literally translates as 'Old Sai loses a horse.' … The expression is used to remind others to take life in stride because things aren't really as good (or bad) as they seem. Certainly seems like wise advice for a society that lives only for the present." With this in mind, using Old Sai's name seemed the most appropriate way to tell the story.

Storytelling Tips

This is one of those stories that the audience loves because they "get" what is happening before the story ends. When telling it, I often ask the audience what Old Sai will respond to his neighbors, thus establishing the give and take that is so important in the actual telling of a story. Since the story is so short, it made a wonderful introduction to a homily I gave at my church.

Tuīqiāo Or Push or Knock

An Ancient Chinese Story Poem about Weighing One's Words

As told through Translator Yan Lixian

Performed by Students
Huai Hai Zhong Road Elementary School, Shanghai

Jia Dao, a poet of the Tang Dynasty, was on his way to the capital city of Chang'an to take the imperial exam which he had failed to pass several times, when night overtook him. He saw in the distance, a Temple in the woods. The moon was full and the evening birds were ending their songs when he arrived. This inspired Jia Dao to write a new poem.

He wrote:"Birds perch in the tree by the pool.
A monk pushes on the door under the moon."

But then he thought, "Which would be better? Should the monk knock on the door or just push it open?"

Since he could not figure out which word would be better he thought, "I'll sleep on it. Wisdom always comes with the first light."

So, he knocked on the Temple door, was admitted by one

of the monks and shown to a room. As he went about getting ready for sleep he kept asking himself, "Push or knock? Knock or push?" accompanied by gestures indicating pushing and knocking.

The next morning he was no wiser than he had been the night before. So after a cup of tea and a little rice, Jia Dao, climbed on his donkey and set out for the city of Chang'an, still trying to decide if he should use the word push or knock.

Han Yu, a famous scholar poet, was a High Official in the capital city of Chang'an. As he was carried through the streets the people were expected to stay out of his way. Everyone did so as drawing near meant being removed by his body guards. The people were also expected to bow down as his sedan chair passed.

The day Jia Dao entered the city he was concentrating on his new poem. And Han Yu was making his way through the City being carried in his sedan chair. Jia Dao was still thinking about the part of his poem that had him stumped. "Should I write 'the monk pushes the door open' or 'the monk knocks at the door?'," he kept asking himself.

And to the amusement of the people in the street, he began acting out the motions of knocking and pushing while he was riding along on his donkey, debating to himself. So intent was he on figuring out which word to use, Jia Dao did not see Han Yu's sedan chair. His donkey jostled Han Yu's carriers, almost causing them to drop the chair. Han Yu was furious. His body guards rushed over to Jia Dao, "You are under arrest!"

The poet pleaded, "I did not see Han Yu coming because I was concentrating so hard on this new poem I am writing."

But the guards took Jia Dao to Han Yu anyway and made him kneel. "Why were you flailing your hands about and not paying attention to your surroundings?" he was asked by Han Yu.

The poet folded his hands, hung his head and pleaded with the High Official, "Please release me. I am merely having a wordy dilemma with this new poem I am writing. The words tuī (push) and qiāo (knock) are swimming in my head and I cannot decide which the better word to use is. I was too involved to think about anything else."

"Recite the poem and maybe I can help," replied Han Yu who also loved to write poetry.

Jia Dao recited:"Birds perch in the tree by the pool.
 A monk knocks on a door under the moon."
"Or do you think the monk should just push the door open?" he asked.

Because he was so intrigued, Han Yu released Jia Dao; and they went off together acting out the gestures in the new poem and discussing the poem as they went. Han Yu favored the word "qiāo" because knocking would awaken the birds making the poem go from tranquil to raucous. From Yin to Yang.

And so the poem reads to this day: "Birds perch in the tree by the pool. A monk knocks on a door under the moon."

Author's Notes

Tuīqiāo is the Chinese expression for "deliberation." Literally the expression means "push or knock on the door" with Tuī meaning push and Qiāo meaning knock. The origin of the expression, the literary legend, is well-known among Chinese writers and shows how Chinese poets have always very carefully chosen the words for their poems, especially when both words seem equal.

"Push or Knock, a vivid literary allusion, has become the standard way to say 'to fuss over wording' in Chinese." (Schrist)

Chang'an is today called Xi'an.

The Imperial Exams were invented during the Han dynasty as a way of sustaining the bureaucracy established during the Qin dynasty. This exam is similar in concept to the civil servant exam administered in the U.S. today. Many second sons took the exams in order to attain status. Scholars, poets and artists were also encouraged to take the exam. The exams have lasted in one form or another to present times. Although they were invented by the Han dynasty, it was the Tang dynasty which made them effective. Exams were given every three years and required years of studying and memorizing Confucian philosophy. Most scholars never reached the highest levels, but were content with being part of the gentry on a local level. The scholar-officials many times were intermediaries between the local communities and the government. (Crozier)

Yin and Yang is an East Asian concept dealing with all aspects of life. Yin is earth, female, dark, passive and absorbing. Valleys, streams and even numbers contain yin. Yang is heaven, male, light, active and penetrating. Mountains and odd numbers contain yang. They represent the interdependence of opposite. (Britannica Concise Encyclopedia)

Storytelling Tips

This story is entertaining and fun to tell with very large motions showing pushing and knocking when Jia Dao is debating with himself either as he readies himself for bed or is riding his donkey through the streets concentrating only on his poem. It helps the listeners see how he could have easily jostled Han Yu's chair. I have the finished poem on a scroll to read at the end of the story.

The students who performed this story for us were dressed in modern clothes – jeans and t-shirts – topped by costumes complete with crepe paper topknots on the two poets. They were very intent upon the serious concept of choosing the best word when writing.

Longevity or Shou

Told by Mr. Wong, Calligraphy teacher at the Jiu Xian Qiao
Community Center in Beijing

An emperor of the Qing Dynasty said to two of his high officials, "Let us leave the Imperial Palace and go walking about the countryside."

They all dressed in plain clothes like the common people wore because the Emperor wanted to find out how his people were faring. It was his way of inspecting the country.

The Emperor was dressed as a merchant. His assistants, Mr. Lui and Mr. He, were also dressed as merchants. First, they walked to the Summer Palace, and from there they ventured into the mountains west of Peking. Wanting to see what the villagers' life was like, they went to a small mountain village where they mixed with people on a street crowded with small, humble homes.

They found a very old woman sitting in front of a gate outside her home. The Emperor asked his assistants, "How old do you think she is?"

Both answered, "She is at least 100 years old!"

So the Emperor called to the Old Woman, "Grandmother, how old are you?"

She answered, "Oh, I am young. Just 141 years."

The Old Woman's hair was tied up in a red ribbon. When the Emperor saw that, he had to ask, "Why are you wearing a red ribbon in your hair?"

With a frown, she replied, "My mother-in-law forces me to wear it for good luck."

"Your mother-in-law? Is she still alive?" asked the astounded Emperor.

"Yes," she sighed.

"May we meet her?" the officials and the Emperor eagerly asked together.

"I'm sorry," replied the Old Woman. "You did not come at the right time. She is not here."

"Where is she?" they asked, now very curious.

"She has gone to visit the great-grandmother of my children," was the reply.

Because the Emperor was so impressed with the Old Woman he composed a poem for her on the spot. The poem said:

"Because you are 141 years old,
You are sixty plus sixty plus twenty-one years,
You are seventy plus seventy plus one winter.
I make you this poem to
Grant you peace."

Author's Notes

Peking is now known as Beijing.

In China asking one's age was not an impolite thing to do – longevity is revered as a sign of wisdom. Still today in China it is a sign of respect to ask someone how old he or she is. Wisdom comes with age and the older you are, the wiser you should be. (Yan)

If you are a visitor in China, you may be asked how old you are; this is a sign showing respect and revering wisdom which comes with age. This happened to one of the women on our tour. She was a spry eighty-year-old with pure white hair. Or you may be asked to guess an elder's age, as happened to me. It is impolite to try and figure out how old the person is by using what they have said.

The color red is considered lucky in China because according to legend, a monster known as Nian showed up at the end of each year attacking villages and eating livestock. Nian was discovered to have three weaknesses –fear of loud noises, hatred of bright light, and loathing for the color red. Thus the Chinese built the customs of celebrating the New Year on the fears of Nian. Firecrackers frightened Nian away, bonfires lit up the night and the color red placed everywhere kept it away. Nian now means New Year and any shade of red is lucky anytime of the year. (Chai)

Storytelling Tips

This is a good story to tell many different age groups and is especially fun with mixed-generational groups. Of course, the Grandmother speaks with an old woman's voice. I always pause after delivering the punch line because it takes some listeners a moment to "get it." When I reach the Emperor's poem I unroll a scroll tied with a red ribbon and read it. Thus I do not have to memorize the poem, and I always have it available when I am telling the story.

The Young Head of the Household

Found on the internet site called "Stories to Grow By"
with Whootie the Owl!
and in several anthologies before and after traveling to China

Once there was an old man who had lost both his mother and his wife. He had four sons and three daughters-in-law. The young women had recently married his three eldest sons. The man thought that none of the young women were very bright and did not want to put any of them in charge of running his household for good reason. Quite often they would come to him asking about things they should have been taught before their marriages.

"Honorable Farther, the chickens are loose from their pens. What should we do?"

"Honorable Father, how do we make rice?"

Not only did they constantly ask questions about daily tasks, the three lonely young women incessantly begged to visit their families in another village when not even a year had passed since their marriages although they had seen their families on the required visit three days following the wedding ceremonies.

"Honorable Father, we miss our families, may we go to visit them today?"

Irritated by their constant complaining, the Old Man came

up with a way to rid himself of the three Young Women. He called them to him and said, "You are always begging me to allow you to go and visit your families. I am not as hard-hearted as you think. You may go, but only upon this condition. When you come back, you will each bring me something I want. One of you shall bring me fire wrapped in paper, the second shall bring me wind in paper, and the third shall bring me music in wind. If you promise to bring me these things, you may go. But if you refuse, you are never to ask me to let you go home again! However, if you go and fail to obtain these gifts for me, you are never to come back!"

The thoughtless Young Women, never once considering how hard their task was, bowed and replied, "Of course Most Honorable Father, we will obtain these gifts for you. Thank you for allowing us to visit our families!" And bowing again, off they went to visit their families in the next village.

As they walked along, they gossiped about the people in their village and decided who they wanted to visit first when they arrived. They had gone quite a way when one young woman's shoe broke. They all sat down on the bank of a stream so that the unfortunate young woman could fix her shoe. While sitting there they began to realize what their father-in-law had asked them to do.

"How can we ever find the things he asked for?" wailed one of the girls.

"Who has even heard of such things?" asked another.

"We will never see our husbands again!" cried the third. This set all of them to weeping hysterically.

While they sat there crying, a Farm Girl riding on the back of her water buffalo came along. "What is the matter?" she asked. "Maybe I can help."

"Oh there is no way you can help us! Just leave us alone!" the Young Women wailed.

"Nothing is ever as bad as it seems," answered the Farm Girl. "Tell me what is troubling you, and let us see if I can help."

So the Young Women sadly told the Farm Girl, "Our Father-in-law expects us to find impossible gifts for him at the market before we are allowed to return to our husbands."

"What gifts is he asking you to find?" the Farm Girl inquired politely.

"I have to bring him fire wrapped in paper!" cried the first Young Woman.

"My gift is to be wind wrapped in paper," sighed the second.

"And me, I am to purchase for him music in the wind! How will we ever find those kinds of gifts?" wailed the third.

As they started weeping again, one of the Young Women held up her broken shoe. "And on top of that I broke my shoe and cannot seem to fix it; so I cannot even go anywhere."

"Well," replied the Farm Girl, "at least fixing your shoe should be easy enough. Come with me." So, all of them set off for the farm with the shoeless Young Woman riding on the back of the water buffalo. Soon they reached the farm where the Farm Girl quickly repaired the shoe. The Young Women were invited to stay the night and gratefully accepted the offer.

That evening the Farm Girl puzzled over the father-in-law's requests. Finally she sprang up and said, "I have it. I know what he wants!" She told the three Young Women what to buy when they reached their village. They thanked her, and the next day on they went.

The Young Women had fun visiting with their families and friends. They also went shopping with their friends at the colorful bustling local open markets where shoppers were offered an amazing array of fresh and crafted items. They purchased the items their father-in-law had requested. When the time came, they returned to their husbands' home.

Meanwhile, the Old Man was satisfied that he had gotten rid of his bothersome daughters-in-law. So when he saw them walking up the road one day, he was quite surprised! He began to yell at them as soon as they could hear him. "What do you mean returning here when there is no way you could have possibly brought the gifts I demanded?"

"But Father," the Young Women replied, "we were able to find exactly what you wanted!" And they produced their packages.

The first took out . . . a paper lantern. "Here is fire wrapped in paper, Father," she said. And indeed, when lit a paper lantern does contain fire.

The second showed him . . . a beautiful fan. "I have brought you wind in paper, Father," she said. She waved the fan producing a delightful breeze.

The third had . . . a set of wind chimes. "Look, Father, here is music in the wind," she said. Just then a playful breeze blew through the chimes producing a lovely sound. The Old Man was astonished and thought to himself, "None of these girls is smart enough to have thought of this by herself. I must find out who told them the answers to my riddles." So he asked, "Who told you what to buy for me?"

The Young Women told him all about the Farm Girl and how she had figured out what he wanted.

The Old Man was so impressed with the intelligence of the Farm Girl that he arranged for her to be married to his youngest son. After the wedding, he told everyone that this extraordinarily wise young woman would become the Head of the Household. Everyone agreed she was the logical choice.

And thus the family lived happily, prospered, and produced many fine grandchildren for the Old Man.

Author's Notes

I unearthed many versions of this tale. Most had a different and longer ending than I have here. I liked this ending for the six through ten year old children I tell the story to since after answering the riddles, the climax, for them, has been reached.

In Old China the "Head of the Household" was the eldest woman living in the household. Usually it was the wife of the eldest man. The Head of the Household was in charge of seeing that the household ran smoothly. She did not have to prepare the meals, shop for food and clothing, clean and do all the other work herself; rather she delegated the work to the other women in the household – other wives, wives of younger men and daughters. (Yan)

When a woman married, she moved in with her husband's family. Except for the prescribed visit three days after her marriage, she was usually not allowed to visit her family until she had been married for at least a year. This was to ensure that she would become used to the ways of her husband's family and forget about how things were done in her former home. Because a new wife was the newest member of the household she was usually given the worst chores, cleaning the kitchen, scrubbing the floors, emptying human waste, to perform. This was the "pecking order" of the household in Old China. (Yan)

Storytelling Tips

This was the story I learned before traveling to China. I really didn't understand the significance of the youngest daughter-in-law becoming the Head of the Household until I arrived in China and asked about this story. I was told that traditionally the newest woman was made to feel inferior because that's what had happened to the mother-in-law when she entered the household. So now I always explain the situation to the listeners before telling the story.

At the point in the story when the young women come home with their packages, I lift up a tapestry bag with three pockets which I purchased in China. Each object has a pocket of its own. Listeners enjoy guessing what the daughters-in-law purchased at the market. I never let on if they are right or wrong, but finally ask, "Would you like to see?" Then I pull out the object we have been discussing.

I needed to purchase the lantern and the fan in China and was able to find them both in the bustling, open markets of Shanghai. The wind chime, I already had. It was given to my family when I was a youngster by my mother's best friend who was a missionary in China. She later disappeared during the Cultural Revolution.

Weaving Fair Lady and Water Buffalo Boy
Or
The Magpie Bridge

Retold by Huáng Kānglè (Sky)
Tour Guide and Translator in Guizhou Province

A young boy once lived in the south of China. His family was very rich and owned much land; but when his parents died, his older brother inherited everything, as was the custom in Old China. The older brother and his wife then threw the young boy out of the house with only an old water buffalo to keep him company.

The Boy and the Water Buffalo found a small cottage where they lived together. They were friends and kept each other company through the long days and nights, so that people started calling the boy Water Buffalo Boy. One day when Water Buffalo Boy had become a young man, the Water Buffalo said, "Would you like to get married?"

Water Buffalo Boy was amazed since the Water Buffalo had never spoken to him before. "You are talking!" he gasped. "Yes, I would like to get married."

"Very well," said the Water Buffalo. "Go to the river where the Star Maidens bathe. Take the pink clothes and run away."

So the next morning Water Buffalo Boy went to the river and followed it through the grasses and green thickets of bamboo until he saw the seven maidens bathing out in the river. Then he took the pink clothes which belonged to the youngest maiden and ran away to hide in a nearby thicket of bamboo.

When the Star Maidens finished their bath, the youngest Star Maiden looked all over for her clothes, but could not find them anywhere. "Have you seen my clothes?" she asked all of her sisters; but none of them could tell her where they were.

Her six sisters got dressed and called to their youngest sister, "Hurry and find your clothes! We must leave without delay! Father is waiting for our return."

When the youngest Star Maiden could not find her clothes anywhere her sisters flew back without her to Heaven where their Heavenly Father, the Jade Emperor, lived.

Finally the youngest Star Maiden spied Water Buffalo Boy in the bamboo thicket holding her clothing and asked him, "Why did you take my clothes?" Feeling ashamed, he said nothing but held out her clothes. She dressed and followed him to his cottage, asking every once and awhile, "Why did you take my clothes?"

Water Buffalo Boy did not answer her for he was too ashamed of what he had done. When they got to the cottage, the youngest Star Maiden asked again, "Why did you take my clothes?"

This time the Water Buffalo answered, "Honorable Star Maiden, he wants to get married."

"Oh," she exclaimed! "I would like that. Thank you Honorable Water Buffalo. And my name is Weaving Fair Lady, because it is my job to weave clouds and rainbows into the sky."

Water Buffalo Boy and Weaving Fair Lady fell in love and married soon after. They were poor, but happy. Eventually the young couple had twin boys whom they loved very much. They lived thus for three earth years. This was a new and very different way of counting time for Weaving Fair Lady since she was accustomed to heavenly days which equal one earth year.

Meanwhile on the heavenly day following the disappearance of the youngest Star Maiden, the Jade Emperor discovered she was missing. The next heavenly day, the third year on earth, he sent other gods to bring her back because without her the heavens were empty and no longer beautiful. After much searching, they found her and pulling her from her husband's and sons' arms, took her back to her father.

Water Buffalo Boy was very sad at the loss of his beautiful wife. She meant everything to him. The little boys missed their mother especially at night when they cried themselves to sleep.

One evening the Water Buffalo said, "Kill me and use my skin to make a basket so you can fly to Heaven with your twin sons and find your wife, Weaving Fair Lady."

But Water Buffalo Boy could not bring himself to kill his old friend, the Water Buffalo. Seeing this, the Water Buffalo lay down, breathed his last breath and died; so that Water Buffalo Boy might find his wife.

Water Buffalo Boy made the baskets from the Water Buffalo's skin which magically took him and his sons to Heaven where he found Weaving Fair Lady. She was glad to see her earthly family, but her Heavenly Father, the Jade Emperor, was angry. He took his knife and split the sky between them, so that Water Buffalo Boy and Weaving Fair Lady could not be together.

Weaving Fair Lady longed to be with her husband and sons. She knew what to do. She called to her friends the magpies, "Come build a bridge for my family and me."

All the magpies came to her aide and made a bridge with their wings across the chasm the Jade Emperor had cut in the sky. Weaving Fair Lady's mother, the Heavenly Queen took pity on them; she said, "Weaving Fair Lady and Water Buffalo Boy you may meet in the middle of the bridge one special night out of the year."

They became the Weaving Fair Lady (Zhi Nu) and Water Buffalo Boy (Niu Lang) Stars. The chasm is the Milky Way, the bridge is the galaxy in between their stars, and once a year in the summer they meet. This is Qi Xi, a Day for Lovers or the Chinese Valentine's Day.

Author's Notes

Water Buffalo Boy translates as Niu Lang, in Chinese, and Weaving Fair Lady in Chinese is Zhi Nu. Westerners know the stars Zhi Nu and Niu Lang, as Vega in the constellation of Lyra east of the Milky Way and Altair in the constellation of Aquila west of the Milky Way. Under the first quarter moon on the seventh day of the seventh lunar month (which usually falls in August), a lighting condition in the sky causes the Milky Way to appear dimmer; and this corresponds to the temporary end to the separation of the two lovers.

A website that includes the lunar calendar and western dates for seven of the Chinese Festivals is http://www.travelchinaguide. com/essential/holidays/. ("Travel China Guide").

"This story has been passed from generation to generation for thousands of years in China. Since it is a very ancient story, there are many different versions. There is nothing wrong with any version because it is a very widely spread story. The versions are basically the same with minor differences in the details. This story actually originates from the worship of stars and constellations. The names occurring in the Chinese version are the names of stars. The story also inspired a lot of poets." (Huang)

In many versions of the story it is the Queen Mother or Heavenly Queen who creates the heavenly river. But in all the versions I have come across, this is a story of unrequited love where the marriage is not arranged. In ancient times this festival was celebrated mainly by girls and women who gave offerings for fertility and happiness in marriage. (Chai)

Storytelling Tips

About mid-way through the process of learning this story, I took a storytelling workshop from Cherie Karo Schwartz. She had us visualize parts of a story we were working on in order to see what we needed to add to the details. The river scene where Water Buffalo Boy steals Weaving Fair Lady's clothes is the scene I imagined. Finally, it made sense to me, and I was able to see where Water Buffalo Boy hid. In my mind the setting became a faint watercolor-like green and it remains that way today when I tell Water Buffalo Boy and Weaving Fair Lady.

I have told this story both during February when the Western Valentine's Day occurs and in August when the stars can be seen in the alignment mentioned in the story.

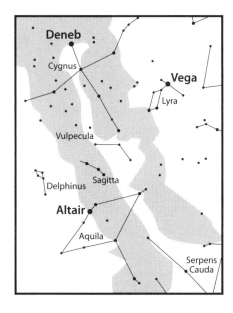

The Butterfly Lovers

Retold by Ms Yan Lixian
National Storytelling Tour Guide

The story is set in the Eastern Jin Dynasty (317-420 CE)

Zhu Yingtai was the only daughter of the prosperous Zhu family. She was rather rambunctious instead of the predictble proper young lady of a well-to-do family because she had only brothers as role models. She also desperately wanted to obtain an education, which of course, was out of the question for a young woman in Old China. She listened outside the door while the tutor taught her brothers and copied the characters they drew; so she knew how to read and write.

Yingtai thought, "I must plan a way to acquire my education."

She cut her hair in the manner of a proper young man and dressed in her brothers' clothing. In order to discover if her disguise would work, she contrived to meet her father away from the home. In two hours' time with her father, she was able to convince him she was a young man. She asked questions about his business and soaked up his answers like a sponge. When she finally revealed who she was her father was shocked and amazed. She had been so convincing that when she pleaded with her parents, "Please allow me to obtain an education so that I may help with your business," her parents reluctantly agreed to allow her to travel to Hangzhou to study with Master Zhou at his boarding school. She would have to remain in disguise as a young man while she studied.

To reach Hangzhou, Yingtai had to walk a long way. On the road she met a young man, Liang Shanbo, who was also on his way to the school of Master Zhou. Shanbo told her, "My family is very poor, but I was able to obtain a scholarship to study with Master Zhou. It is an honor for one such as I to be allowed to study."

Yingtai replied, "It doesn't matter to me that your family is poor, perhaps we can travel together and pass the time by talking." Liang Shanbo and Zhu Yingtai became good friends on their journey.

Although Yingtai hid her identity well, she soon began to fall in love with Shanbo. She thought, "I can never reveal myself or I will immediately be dismissed from school." So she contented herself with friendship which soon developed into the closeness of brothers. The two friends went to classes together, studied together, ate together, walked together, and talked about many things as they became closer. Yingtai was sad that she could not reveal her true identity.

One day Yingtai received a letter from her father which explained "Your mother is gravely ill, and you are needed at home at once!"

She showed the letter to Shanbo as she was packing her few belongings. He felt very sorry for her and said, "You should not have to go alone. I will travel with you at least part of the way."

Yingtai was grateful for his company and thought, "Perhaps I can tell him who I really am on the way home."

As they walked along, Yingtai thought, "I will subtly tell him I am a girl."

When they paused by a lake, she pointed out two Mandarin ducks, which in China are a symbol of lovers. "Look, two ducks, just like us!" she exclaimed.

"No!" laughed Shanbo. "We are brothers--not lovers!"

Further along, they stopped under a lotus tree. Looking up, Yingtai saw two blossoms growing very close together from one stem. "Look," she said, "two lotus blossoms, just like us!"

"No!" replied Shanbo. "We are brothers--not lovers!"

Still further along, while walking through a field, Yingtai saw two doves flying together. "Look, two doves, just like us!"

"No! We are brothers not lovers!" He just did not understand what she was trying to explain.

Finally, exasperated, Yingtai said, "You know Shanbo; I have a 'sister' of marriageable age. Would you like to meet her?"

"If she's half as nice as you, her brother, it would be the best marriage possible! And we would really be brothers," replied Shanbo.

Now Yingtai in her role as a young man of the family was entitled to arrange a marriage for her "sister". So Yingtai invited Shanbo to come all the way home with her, which pleased him greatly.

When they reached Yingtai's home, Shanbo was invited to spend the night. The next morning he met Yingtai's "sister" and thought, "She is as wonderful as my friend and very beautiful!" He fell in love. Yingtai, dressed as her "sister," felt her heart leap for joy.

Her joy was short lived, for after Shanbo left, Yingtai's mother revealed, "I am not really ill."

The letter had been a ruse to get Yingtai home so she could be wed to a rich man her father knew through his business, a marriage which her parents had arranged for her. Since Shanbo, the love of her life, was from a poor family, Yingtai knew her parents would never agree to a marriage between them. She was very sad.

When Shanbo next came to visit, Yingtai, as her "sister", had to tell him, "I cannot see you again." It broke her heart to say that, but there was nothing else she could do. She could not explain everything that was happening.

Shanbo was very upset. He had hoped for a bride, but now he was turned away. He became very depressed thinking of his situation as he made his way back to school. He missed his friend and had no one to whom he could talk. He could not study, he could not eat, he just sat in his room missing his "brother" more than ever. And he wondered why the "sister" had turned him away when he had hoped to make her his bride. Things became so bad Shanbo decided he had nothing to live for. He died of a broken heart.

As was the custom in Old China, Liang Shanbo's tomb was set on a hillside near a lovely little stream with trees growing nearby to ensure good feng shui. This was near Yingtai's town. When she heard the news, Yingtai cried everyday whenever she was alone. There was nothing else she could do until she started planning again.

She told her parents, "I am placing three conditions on going through with this marriage. One, I must be allowed to wear white beneath my bright red wedding gown. Two, I must be allowed to take the road which leads by Shanbo's tomb on my way to the wedding at my new husband's home. Three, I must be allowed to stop at Shanbo's tomb to pay my respects to my old friend."

Although her parents weren't happy about consenting to her conditions, they agreed because otherwise she refused to go through with the marriage. This would never do as the family would lose face.

The day of her wedding came. Yingtai dressed very

carefully. She wore a white gown, the color of mourning in China, under her exquisite, bright red wedding gown. The bearers hoisted her sedan chair to their shoulders and set off down the road to Shanbo's tomb. Her chair was set down; carefully she alighted and made her way to the tomb. There she removed the red gown to reveal her beautiful white dress. She placed flowers at the tomb, fell to her knees and began to weep.

She cried for a long time. While she was weeping thunderclouds gathered. Rain poured down, thunder crashed, lightning lit the sky. A bolt of lightning struck Shanbo's tomb. It split open. Yingtai instantly made a decision. She threw herself into the open tomb. The tomb suddenly closed. Yingtai and Shanbo were together.

The stunned wedding party stood there and gasped in horror. They could not believe their eyes. The bride was gone and there was absolutely nothing they could do except go explain to the rich man who was to have been her husband. However, no one wanted to do that; so they stayed by the tomb. When the rain stopped and the sun reappeared everything seemed clean and fresh. As they watched, two beautiful butterflies flew from a hole in the top of the sealed tomb.

Shanbo ~ and Yingtai ~ together ~ forever!

Author's Notes

In Old China, fathers were not close to their daughters. It was sons a father desired. Yingtai would never consider going against her parents matrimonial wishes because that would make them "lose face," the ultimate disgrace, as "face" is the public persona which includes one's dignity and public identity. (Chai) She could be disinherited or shunned. Instead she honored her parents by agreeing to the marriage they had planned for her. However in this story which has become a favorite Chinese opera,

Yingtai finds a way to make her wishes known, to begin obtaining her education and to find a place with her lover instead of going through with the marriage her parents had arranged for her.

Feng shui, literally wind water, is an eastern concept of living in harmony with our surroundings and nature instead of trying to control them. Harmony and balance comes from the Daoist philosophy. (Chai) It was considered the best feng shui to have a burial tomb on a hillside where there were trees and a stream or river flowing by. If a tomb was built in the wrong place, it could affect the family for three generations. (Yan) Still today in the rural areas of China you can see tombs on the hillsides.

Storytelling Tips

When I first told Butterfly Lovers to a group of elders, they loved it. The first thing I asked them before starting the story was, "Do you remember your very first love?" There were many nods and some misty eyes. By the time the story was finished, everyone's eyes were misty and some actually had tears running down their faces.

Older students also like this story, especially if they have any knowledge of Shakespeare's Romeo and Juliet. Their prior knowledge opens the door to a comparison of the two stories. Butterfly Lovers is actually much older than Romeo and Juliet as it is set in the Eastern Jin Dynasty of China (317-420 CE), while Romeo and Juliet was written during the 1590's about a couple who lived in the 1290's and early 1300's. With the students I will often play music from the Chinese Opera, Butterfly Lovers in the background as I tell the story to set the mood. This is also how I tell Butterfly Lovers on the radio.

As the butterflies emerge from the top of the tomb, I use my hands to symbolize a butterfly flying away. And very slowly say the words, "Shanbo ~ and Yingtai ~ together ~ forever!"

Tears that Crumbled the Great Wall

Retold by Dr. Kang Li of the China Folklore Society
Translated by Ms Yan Lixian, National Storytelling Tour Guide

During the beginning of the Qin Dynasty, the first Emperor, who called himself Qin Shi Huangdi, wanted to rebuild and connect the walls built to protect the Warring States from invasions by the nomadic Hsiung Nu tribes from the north. This was no easy task. The border was long and treacherous winding through the mountainous regions in northern China. So in order to have enough laborers, he conscripted many of the male population by force. Qin Shi Huangdi's soldiers forced the conscripted men to march the long distance to the Wall where they were given no warm clothing and very little food. His subjects began to hate him. Families hid their sons, men tried to find ways to hide for no one wanted to help build the Great Wall under the severe conditions being reported back to them. Very little food and rest were provided for the laborers. When they starved or froze to death their bodies were left to lie about and then buried in the next section of the Wall.

It is no wonder that Fan Xiliang, a scholar, wanted to find a place to hide. Running away from the soldiers, he pushed through a hedge surrounding the gardens of Meng Jiang's family where she was working. Before she could cry out, he explained, "I am running away from the soldiers who want to conscript me to build the Great Wall! Please allow me to hide myself here."

Meng Jiang took pity upon poor Fan Xiliang. With her parents consent, he was allowed to go into hiding although they knew the penalties for hiding an able-bodied man were stiff and could include death. Every day Meng Jiang provided food and companionship. The couple soon fell in love. Meng Jiang's parents granted them permission to marry. But no sooner had the ceremony taken place, than the soldiers pounded on the door, demanding to see the bridegroom. Pulling him from Meng Jiang's arms they dragged Fan Xiliang away.

Many months passed with no word of how Fan Xiliang was faring. Meng Jiang was saddened when she thought, "How cruel Qin Shi Huangdi is, forcing men to be torn from their families and toil under harsh conditions just to satisfy his need to be mighty. I hate him so much! But I miss my husband even more." With that thought she burst into tears.

It was spring, the gardens were in full bloom, the swallows flew in pairs looking for places to build their nests. Meng Jiang felt the pangs of loneliness all day and night. She longed for her husband, to regain the loving companionship they had shared. All summer she reminisced about their discussions, walks in the secluded gardens and sharing meals as she worked in the gardens she waited for news. No news ever came.

The falling leaves in autumn made her think of tears falling from heaven for her husband and all the other thousands of men whom the soldiers tore from the arms of their families as ordered by the cruel Emperor. She heard the rumors every time she went out.

"The men who were taken from our village are forced to work so hard every day, all day."

"How little food they are given to eat; and their clothes, they are threadbare because they have nothing but what they were wearing the day the left."

"The cold north wind is so bitter it seems to freeze your bones."

Someone even told her, "It is so cold when the men take their hands from their sleeves to work frostbite sets in."

That night, Meng Jiang dreamed her husband was calling out to her, "I am cold, so unbearably cold!"

So in the morning she began making cotton padded clothing, heavily padded shoes, padded mitts and a winter coat for him. "But who?" she thought, "Who should take these clothes to him? No one wants to go for fear of never coming back." Finally she decided, "I will take them myself!"

By the time Meng Jiang started out to find Fan Xiliang, all the leaves had fallen from the trees, the harvest was in and the ground was bare. Her walk was lonely, forlorn and dismal. She had never been far from her home and did not know exactly where she was going except that she had heard the Wall was being built in the North. Whenever she met someone along the way, she asked, "Which way to the Wall? How much further must I go?"

A few people she met told her, "Go North. The Wall is far."

Some said, "The cold will show you the way. You have a long journey ahead."

While others just shook their heads sadly and pointed North.

Because the days were growing shorter, one evening she failed to reach the next town before nightfall. She found a small temple in a grove of trees by the side of the road and decided to sleep there for the night. She was so very tired that she fell asleep as soon as she lay down upon the stone table. That night she dreamed again.

As Fan Xiliang floated toward her, a feeling of great

happiness enveloped her. She reached her arms out toward him wanting to touch his skin. But he said in an eerie voice, "I am no longer living . . ."

Meng Jiang cried bitter tears when she woke, realizing that what she had dreamed was probably true. "How can I continue? What's the use?" she asked herself. "No, I must go on, for if my husband is dead, then I must recover his bones and give him a proper funeral or he will never rest peacefully, and neither will I-- knowing I could have done this for him."

Her determination renewed, Meng Jiang started out once again. A week later she came to a small inn by the side of the hilly road. The old woman who ran it asked, "What is a young girl like yourself doing out here all alone in this cold winter?"

She listened respectfully as Meng Jiang told her story which moved her to tears. Drying her eyes she uttered, "How cruel our emperor is! The Wall is still so far away over mountains and rivers! You are so weak and tired from your long and arduous journey. How will you go on?"

"I must," Meng Jiang stated resolutely.

The old woman saw she could not persuade Meng Jiang to stay with her through the long, cold winter. Touched by Meng Jiang's determination, and worried about the younger woman's safety, yet understanding that she must go on the old woman declared, "I will walk a ways with you offering companionship and protection from predators as best I can."

When they parted the old woman gave her an extra measure of millet and soybeans wrapped in cabbage leaves, a warm jacket and some advice. "Don't give up your quest. You must find out what has happened to your young husband and give the people hope. Perhaps even the Emperor will see the error of his ways, but I rather doubt that."

After her visit with the old woman, Meng Jiang was lonelier

than before. The way was rough, the wind icy cold. Meng Jiang forced her swollen feet to move one step at a time, thinking only about the love she possessed for her husband.

A few days later she came to the mouth of a deep valley with high mountains on either side. It was a gray, overcast day. The snow clouds rode low in the sky and the wind shrieked mockingly. On Meng Jiang went, not seeing anything that was alive, just barren hillsides with jagged rocks. When it was so dark she could no longer see the road, she heard running water and decided there might be some protection from the wind nearby. She found a few bushes to curl up in and was soon fast asleep. She had not eaten all day, and as she slept the cold crept into her bones. She shivered violently when she thought about the suffering her husband was surely enduring. In the morning she woke to a dazzling, white world. Snow blanketed everything including herself.

"How will I ever be able to find my way now?" she wondered.

Just then she saw a crow swoop down nearby. It cawed twice and flew off, only to return and repeat its behavior. "Are you my guide?" she asked.

The crow flew off, looking back at her. It waited while she brushed the snow from herself and stretched. By following the patient crow, she was able to resume her journey. It cheered her a little to have the companionship of another living thing. Although, she got no replies, she could speak her thoughts aloud as if she were talking to a friend. "I am so tired, but I must go on. My husband needs me and the pants, shoes, coat and mitts that I bring to warm him. If I am cold, how cold must he be? The road is rough, but I dare not rest until night. I wonder how much further we must go?"

Day by day, the crow led her past mountains, through rivers and streams, and over rocks. At last they reached the Great Wall. She whispered, "It looks like a great serpent wriggling through the mountains. Thank you, Kind Crow, for guiding my footsteps."

As she gazed around her, she saw barren mountains, snow, dry grasses, but no trees. People were huddled by the Wall. "They must be the workers," she said as she quickly bade good-bye to her guide. Hurriedly, she ran toward them, eager to ask about her husband.

But no one knew who he was. He was not among the workers here. She still had further to go. "Be brave!" she told herself soundly. "Surely someone will know where he is or what has happened to him.

So resolutely she walked forward once again, this time following the Wall. Whenever she found groups of workers she eagerly asked, "Do you know my husband, Fan Xiliang? Have you seen him anywhere?"

No one had any useful information, but they all sympathized with her plight. Every face she looked into urged her to keep looking. On and on she went. When at last she reached the site where her husband had worked, men with sad eyes told her the tragic news, "Your husband whose poetic words painted pictures of joy in our minds was one of the thousands who died of starvation. His corpse is buried under the Wall."

Meng Jiang had seen the dead and dying men lying on the frozen ground. She had a vision of her husband lying there until his skeleton was shoveled into a trench, the foundation of a new section of the Wall. It was too much for her to bear. She might have gone mad with grief except she remembered what the old woman had told her. Meng Jiang's hatred of the cruel Emperor grew with each bitter tear she shed. She wept a torrent of tears over several days, and many of the workers wept with her.

Suddenly an explosive sound was followed by silence. Everyone instinctively looked at the Wall. Just then the Wall shook violently and began to crumble. Bricks and stones, earth and mortar rained down. People ran screaming to safety. When it was over, the amazed onlookers began saying, "It was the tears of Meng Jiang that crumbled the Wall! Now she can find her husband's bones."

It is said that the gods took pity upon poor Meng Jiang and caused the mighty Wall to crumble for hundreds of miles. Finally, Meng Jiang was able to find her husband's broken body.
All she wanted was to take it home with her for a proper burial.

All along the Wall the workers, when they heard the story of Meng Jiang's long, arduous journey and how her tears brought down the Great Wall, were filled with hatred for the cruel Emperor, Qin Shi Huangdi. "He has brought us nothing but misery!"

The Emperor himself heard how part of his Great Wall had fallen when some poor wretched woman began crying. "What kind of a person—a mere woman—could have caused part of my Great Wall to collapse," he wondered. The Emperor had to see Meng Jiang for himself. At the head of his army, the Emperor set off for the spot where the Wall had collapsed. There, he found Meng Jiang just starting on her journey home. He was taken by her stark beauty and wanted her for himself. Ever so politely he said, "I would like to make you one of my Imperial Wives. Will you accept my magnanimous offer?"

Meng Jiang felt all her hatred rise, her stomach roiled; but calmly she replied, "Yes, on three conditions."

At first the Emperor was taken aback at such an affront, but he did so want her to be his. He inquired, "Anything. What are your conditions?"

"First, there must be a proper burial of my husband's bones in our hometown so that he may rest peacefully. Second, you and all your ministers must attend the funeral dressed in mourning as if Fan Xiliang had been your own son. Third, you must build a monument to my husband and the other workers here at the site where his bones were found"

The Emperor consented; as he wanted Meng Jiang to be his. He arranged for Fan Xiliang's body to be transported back to the village. On the day of the funeral, he dressed in his mourning clothes and walked closely behind the golden coffin. All his generals, ministers and courtiers followed. Later when the monument had been erected and was to be dedicated, the Emperor and all the dignitaries gathered around. The ceremony was short as the Emperor could not wait to make Meng Jiang his. However, she said, "I wish to have a few private moments with the memories of my husband and then I shall ban them from my mind forever."

The Emperor was frustrated, but honored her request. The anticipation of having her for himself with no hint of her former husband's shadow calmed him. Meng Jiang threw herself onto the ground beside the monument and wept bitterly. When she arose she walked gracefully to the edge of a nearby cliff and threw herself into the abyss.

Her white mourning gown billowed around her as she descended without a sound.

Author's Notes
The Wall

In China the Great Wall is called Wan-Li Qang-Qeng which means 10,000 Li Long Wall. It was built in bits and pieces. During the Warring States Period, the kings of the northern states built along parts of their northern borders to protect their kingdoms from invasion by the nomadic tribes wandering the steppes. The short-lived Qin Dynasty, which united all of the Warring States under one king who called himself, Qin Shi Huangdi, oversaw the great undertaking to connect and refortify all of the existing pieces of the Wall. Later in the Ming Dynasty, the Great Wall was enlarged to its present day length with watch towers and cannons for extra protection. It snakes its way from the Jiayu Pass in Gansu Province in the west, to the mouth of the Yalu River in Liaoning Province in the east which is about 4,000 miles. ("Just Travel China")

We climbed the Great Wall at the Ju Yong Guan Pass Section, which is part of the northeastern section just outside Beijing. We were told that President Clinton visited the Wall at the same place. It is the desire of every Chinese to visit the Great Wall before they die. We saw people of all ages and physical descriptions while we were there. For some just touching a piece of the Wall is enough. For others, climbing to the highest point makes their journey worthwhile. We were given a certificate stating in both Chinese and English that we had climbed the Great Wall as part of the People to People National Storytelling Network Delegation.

The Wall is difficult to climb. Some of the steps are no more than a few inches high and others seemed to be almost three feet high. It is especially difficult through the turns and twists where the Wall narrows and the steps are steep. A handrail has been added as a modern convenience. These architectural configurations are not accidents. Everything was done to thwart the enemy from using the Wall to their advantage.

The Story

Tears that Crumbled the Great Wall is known by several titles. I chose the one that most appealed to a sense of the dramatic. For a woman to undertake such a long and arduous journey as Meng Jiang's was an incredible occurrence. The story does not say whether Meng Jiang had bound feet, but if she did such a journey would have put her in terrible pain with each step. The loyalty and perseverance she shows from her first step to her last is an intense journey of devotion and love. Most women in Old China had their marriages arranged for them; and if love came, it came later in the marriage. Devotion and loyalty were prized qualities in a woman.

Taking Fan Xiliang's bones to their ancestral home to be buried ensured that he would rest at peace and not haunt the land looking for his home. Thousands of men who built the Great Wall had no such burial. Their families were not able to perform the traditional ceremonies preparing the dead for their continued existence and well being. Therefore the men who are buried in the Great Wall were not able to "influence the fortune" of their living relatives. (Religion Facts)

The white gown Meng Jiang wears to the funeral and the dedication of the monument is the Chinese traditional color of mourning. She commits suicide at the end of the story because she prefers death over marriage to the Emperor who caused so much hardship and grief.

Storytelling Tips

This story is not only a love story, but it also proves to modern day listeners the horrors of the conditions under which the Great Wall was built. The group I am telling to determines the emphasis I place on either the love story or the conditions surrounding the building of the Great Wall. Elementary students who may be studying Asia are interested in how the Great Wall was built, not so much in a "mushy" love story. But the story is the vehicle to explain what happened. With older students and adults, I usually place more emphasis on the love story aspect.

Timing and pauses are especially important when telling Tears that Crumbled the Great Wall. Fan Xiliang's sudden appearance, the dreams of Meng Jiang, the old woman's great hatred for the Emperor, the appearance of the patient Crow, the explosion, Meng Jiang's jumping off the cliff all have an element of surprise and the audience needs a moment to contemplate what just happened.

The Legend of the White Snake
Also known as
Lady White

Adapted by Julie Herrera

Retold by Dr. Kang Li of the China Folklore Society

Once, two spirit sisters, White Snake and Green Snake practiced Qì for a thousand years in the mysterious E Mei Mountains near Chengdu in Sichuan province. Finally they obtained magical power and were able to transform shapes; and so they choose a human form. The snake girls named themselves Su-Zheng and Xiao Qing. They traveled to West Lake of Hangzhou City in the province of Zhejiang because they were attracted by the beauty they saw and because White Snake remembered a young boy who had saved her life in the area. It was there they met Xu Xian, a young man who was working for a pharmacist.

Su-Zheng felt he may be the man who used to be the boy she was looking for. She used her magical powers to discover if this were true. It was. She was overjoyed, for now she would be able to repay his kindness.

Xu Xian was looking for a boatman to carry him across West Lake. So Su-Zheng and Xiao Qing decided to ask for a ride too. Since there was only one boatman, Xu Xian shared the boat with the two lovely young women.

Su-Zheng nudged her sister and quietly asked her, "Xiao Qing, do you think you could conjure up a rain storm while we are crossing the lake so we may meet with Xu Xian again?" Xiao Qing obliged.

Xu Xian offered his umbrella to the women and said, "Please use my umbrella to keep you dry. Tomorrow I will meet you at the Duan-Qiao Bridge, where we met today, so you can give it back to me."

The next day all three met on the Duan-Qiao Bridge. Su-Zheng, also known as Lady White, was falling in love with Xu Xian; so she convinced her sister to arrange a marriage.

Xiao Qing asked, "Xu Xian, are you married?"

"No," he replied.

"My sister is not married either; perhaps the two of you should marry."

Xu Xian was pleased with the suggestion for he was also falling in love with Su-Zheng. But the Laws of Heaven forbid marriage between a human and a spirit. Even though Su-Zheng knew this, she loved Xu Xian so much that she just had to marry him. And thus the marriage took place.

Su-Zheng provided her husband with a medicine shop. While she wrote out the prescriptions, Xu Xian and Xiao Qing gathered the herbs and dispensed the herbal medicines. Patients who were unable to pay were given free treatment and medicine. Using her magical powers, Su-Zheng caused the herbal medicines to be especially potent, and as a result their business became very popular and prospered.

However, success meant that many people who would normally pray for a cure at the Jin Shan Temple or Temple of Golden Hill did not go to the Temple. Temple donations declined from month to month. FaHai, the head monk of the Temple who also had magical powers, pretended to be a customer at the pharmacy. "Good Day, Madame Su-Zheng. I have need of your services."

Su-Zheng prescribed the medicines FaHai pretended to need. Through his magical insight FaHai knew Su-Zheng and her sister were spirits, incarnations of supernatural snakes. Since it was he who had tried to kill the White Snake long ago, he devised a scheme to get rid of Su-Zheng and Xiao Qing.

FaHai invited Xu Xian to visit the Temple of the Golden Hill. When Xu Xian arrived, FaHai told him, "Your wife and her sister are supernatural snakes! You should not have married her!"

"No," protested Xu Xian, "she is as human as you or I."

"Ha," replied FaHai, "you'll see. She may love you enough not to hurt you intentionally, but you will surely get poisoned through close contact with her."

"Liar!" shouted Xu Xian as he left.

As the time of the Dragon Boat Festival, which takes place on the fifth day of the fifth lunar month, was drawing near, Su-Zheng told her husband, "I am pregnant."

They both rejoiced at the coming of their child. However, Su-Zheng was fearful, for during the Dragon Boat Festival, people would put out herbs such as calamus and mugwort to ward off spirits, and they drank wine made bitter with realgar, a type of arsenic, to keep spirits away. Su-Zheng kept to herself and told her husband, "Since I am pregnant, I do not want to go out to celebrate the Dragon Boat Festival."

FaHai, still determined to get rid of Su-Zheng and her sister, cast a spell over Xu Xian the next time he was at the Temple. Then he politely told Xu Xian, "For the Dragon Boat Festival, prepare the bitter wine made with realgar for your wife. It is beneficial for pregnancies and will ensure that your child is not harmed by evil spirits."

But FaHai knew this would make Su-Zheng reveal her true self. When Xu Xian presented her with the wine, Su-Zheng wanted to refuse the drink, but could think of no reason worth giving that she could not drink it. And so, believing in her superior powers, she drank the wine. It made her so sick that she barely managed to stumble to her bed.

Xu Xian fearing for his wife's health and that of their child ran after her and drew back the bedside curtain. There on the bed was coiled a large white python! The shock of seeing that huge snake killed Xu Xian.

As soon as the realgar had worn off, Su-Zheng returned to her human form. When she saw what had happened to Xu Xian, she was heartbroken. She called to her sister, "Come with me to the Kunlun Mountain so we can steal some lingzhi and bring Xu Xian back to life."

They encountered Brown Deer and White Crane and the other heavenly guards responsible for protecting the lingzhi mushroom, a celestial herb which grew on the Kunlun Mountain. A battle ensued. Su-Zheng and Xiao Qing were losing the battle, when suddenly the voice of the Immortal of the Southern End commanded, "Stop!"

Weeping, Su-Zheng told him what had happened. "I beg you to help me save my human husband!"

Impressed by her sincerity and perseverance, the Immortal gave her the lingzhi so she could bring her husband back from death.

Su-Zheng took the herb home, where she ground it and gave it to Xu Xian. He was revived but still fearful of what he had seen, so he asked Su-Zheng, "Where were you? All I could see was a huge white snake!"

Su-Zheng made up a story. "A dragon descended from

heaven – a good omen for our unborn child. It is too bad we were both unconscious at the time and could not burn incense for the dragon."

After Xiao Qing corroborated the story, Xu Xian believed what he had been told.

In the meantime, FaHai was not satisfied. He told Xu Xian, "Your wife is lying to you to save herself and her unborn spirit child. Save yourself! Get rid of her!"

"No, she is my wife. The child she is carrying is mine. I do not believe you!" retorted Xu Xian.

So FaHai cast a spell over Xu Xian making him move to Jin Shan Temple and become a monk. Su-Zheng was furious. She and Xiao Qing called upon the sea spirits, "Help us save Xu Xian!"

Together with the sea spirits, they raised the water level of West Lake to engulf the Temple; but FaHai used his magic to raise the Temple above the water. This happened several times before Su-Zheng felt her strength fade. She could not keep fighting FaHai. She needed her strength to save her unborn child.

Su-Zheng and Xiao Qing fled to the Duan-Qiao Bridge on West Lake, where they first met Xu Xian. Xiao Qing was very angry at Xu Xian for his unfaithfulness. "I will kill him! He is no good!"

While the sisters wondered what they should do, a young monk secretly released Xu Xian from the Temple, and he also returned to the Duan-Qiao Bridge. When she saw him coming, Xiao Qing wanted to attack Xu Xian, but Su-Zheng told her, "No, I love him. He did not know what he was doing; he was under a spell."

Turning to Xu Xian she told him, "I love you! I really am a spirit who has practiced Qì for 1000 years. Soon our baby will be born. Please let us be a family"

Since she was being truthful, Xu Xian forgave her and they

went home. Soon she gave birth to a son and everyone was very happy. Life seemed to return to normal.

But FaHai was not giving up. He attacked the weakened Su-Zheng and imprisoned her eternally in the Leifeng Pagoda, known as Thunder Peak Pagoda by West Lake.

Xiao Qing fled to practice her magic. Years later her magic was strong enough to take the revenge she so badly wanted. This time Xiao Qing defeated FaHai and had him swallowed by a crab.

Xiao Qing told Su-Zheng's son about his mother's imprisonment. She was finally rescued by her son, when he caused the Leifeng Pagoda to collapse. Thus, Su-Zheng was reunited with her husband, her son and her sister. They all lived happily except for FaHai who is still an old crab.

Author's Notes
The Story

After practicing Qi through meditation, discipline and the mastery of the forces of the universe for a thousand years, it is told a spirit animal can earn the power to shift into human form. (Kang)

The Legend of the White Snake has been told in many versions through the years and is a very popular opera in China today. It is said that the story originated in the Tang Dynasty (618-907 CE). During the Song Dynasty (960-1279 CE), the scenes of West Lake and Thunder Pagoda were added to the story. The story was completed during the Ming Dynasty (1368-1644 CE). Finally during the Qing Dynasty (1644-1911 CE) the legendary story of the White Snake Lady was rewritten, and the characters were made beautiful in order to form the love story now often performed as an opera. ("Chinese Fortune Calendar")

The western name of the life giving herb, lingzhi, is ganoderma. Interestingly, in 2011, I met a woman on a plane who had just attended a conference for her company. She told me she sold coffees and tea laced with ganoderma. "Oh," I replied, "the life giving herb." She was amazed that I had heard of ganoderma or lingzhi. So I told her the story of Lady White, which she had never heard before.

Lingzhi has been used for over 4,000 years in Chinese medicine and is considered a complete herb, to which many healing properties are attributed. Lingzhi mushrooms, also known as glossy ganoderma, have been proven to have both anti-bacterial and anti-viral properties due to ganodermic acid. They may also aid in lowering blood pressure, have beneficial effects on cancerous tumors and protect the liver. (Manal)

The Dragon Boat Festival

Racers paddle boats ranging from forty to one hundred feet in length in a fierce competition. There may be as many as eighty rowers in one boat. The festival's origins were to honor the spirit of the water dragon which is the most powerful and essential of all the Chinese dragons. The festival now also honors Qu Yuan who was a poet scholar from the third century BCE. His advice to the corrupt king was not heeded, so he threw himself into the Milo River. The locals were not able to save him. They threw rice into the river to keep the fish from eating his body which is why an important festival food is flavored glutinous rice wrapped in bamboo leaves and known as zonzi. (Chai)

The Pagoda

The Lei Feng Pagoda was constructed during the Song Dynasty in 975 CE. The Lei Feng suffered a severe disaster during the Ming Dynasty. During the Jiaqing years (1522-1566 CE) Japanese invaders set fire to the pagoda. Finally, in August, 1924, the foot of the pagoda was hollowed out and other parts of the pagoda were so severely damaged by vandalism that suddenly the ancient pagoda collapsed. In November, 2000, the Hangzhou Municipal People's Government stated that it would rebuild Lei Feng Pagoda. The construction was completed in October, 2002. ("Seeraa International")

Storytelling Tips

Because of the complexity of the plot of The White Snake, it is difficult to learn, and of all the Chinese tales, it has taken me the longest. Also, because of the plot line, the story is better suited to older groups of children, young adults, and adults. An explanation of Qì and the concept that animal spirits could shape shift is vital to the understanding of the story.

Much of my understanding of the story comes more from research to find various versions of the story than from the discussions we had in China with the folklorists who told us about this particular story. My notes include a very brief recounting of the story and the book I received is written entirely in Chinese. I would not have included The White Snake except that the concept of Qi and animals shape shifting into other forms intrigues me.

Across the Bridge Rice Noodles
or
Guo Qiao Mi Xian

Adapted by Judith Heineman
from a retelling by Ms Yan LiXin
National Storytelling Tour Guide

A long time ago in Kunming, City of Eternal Spring, where the climate is always temperate, lush vegetables grew and animals were plentiful. Farmers tilled their land far from their homes. One such farmer had to cross a bridge each day to get to his plot of land. His wife loved him very much. She felt it was her duty to bring him a hot lunch each day to keep his strength up while he toiled from early morning until dusk.

She too, started her preparations in the early morning, chopping vegetables and slicing meat so thin that one could see through it. She boiled the bones of old chickens, ducks, and pigs for many hours so that the broth would be healthful. The clearer the broth, the more skill she displayed. When the soup was ready she added her ingredients and off she went, crossing the wooden bridge on her way to bring lunch to her husband. However, by the time she arrived, his lunch was always cold. She felt ashamed.

"How can I bring my worthy husband the hot lunch he deserves?" she thought.

"I shall wrap my coat around the container to keep it warm," she said out loud. She tried this method, but the lunch was cold when she arrived.

"Perhaps if I run across the old wooden bridge my husband's lunch will remain hot!" But even though she ran as fast as she could over the old wooden bridge, the food was still cold when she arrived. She tried not to show her disappointment and her husband never scolded her or frowned, but she knew in her heart that he would have enjoyed a hot meal much more.

One day, she put a hen in the steaming broth and went about her chores. By the time she came back to check on the soup, a thick layer of chicken fat had completely sealed the top of the soup. No steam escaped, but she felt it to be scalding hot. She carefully put all the ingredients into individual containers, including the rice noodles she made that morning, and carried them separately from the soup. This time, when she came to her husband, the soup was piping hot! She could see the pleased look on his face and she was glad.

She spread out a cloth, opened the container, broke the seal of fat that had congealed on top of the soup, and with her chopsticks, she carefully began to add the slices of meat and bits of raw fish. She deftly swished them back and forth a few times until they were cooked right in the soup. Next, she added the vegetables: leeks, "swish," cabbage hearts, "swish," peas, mung bean sprouts, onions and some spices. "Swish, swish!" Lastly, she grabbed the thin rice noodles with her chopsticks and swirled them through the juicy broth. She deftly flicked her delicate wrists so that the noodles twirled in the glistening broth as though they were dancing. The aroma was so fresh and the meal so nutritious that her husband was revived.

The wife carefully packed her bundles and started walking home. When she got to the bridge she turned and waved. She could feel the warmth of her husband's happiness and satisfaction on his face. "Oh, his smile is as warm as the dish I have finally been able to bring to him," she thought as she crossed back over the wooden bridge with a lighter step.

Soon word spread to all the other wives in this village and they too began to prepare their husbands' lunches in the same manner. They let a film of oil seal the top of the soup before they left the house. Then they mixed in the meat, vegetables and lastly the rice course when they arrived at their husbands' sides. By the time all the ingredients were cooked, the soup was cool enough to eat. All the husbands had hot lunches from that time forward and all the wives were considered to be very loving and very clever.

Author's Notes

Judith Heineman, along with Julie Herrrera, was a delegate on the NSN People to People Storytelling Delegation to China in 2008. After the main delegation departed for the states, Judith continued her journey to Kunming and Xi'an. This version of Across the Bridge Rice Noodles was adapted by Judith from a version told to her by Yan Lixian while waiting in the Beijing airport for Judith's flight to Kunming. Earlier when Yan Lixian, translator and national guide for the storytelling delegation, learned Judith was continuing to Kunming, she told Judith she must try this region's national dish, "Across the Bridge Rice Thread Noodles." It can be a poor student's dish, but the more money one has, the more ingredients one can order for the soup! Naturally, Judith asked if there was a story behind this. Yan Lixian obliged by telling her the outline of the story.

As Judith discovered, a visit to Kunming, City of Eternal Spring, in China's southwestern Yunnan Province would not be complete without tasting one of its most renowned dishes. "Across the Bridge Rice Noodles" is made even more savory when one knows the love story responsible for this delicacy.

Judith and her husband's first meal in Kunming was this dish. She recounts: The waitress brought us a bowl of broth with noodles. At our table she added each ingredient in front of us until the bowl was full. It was a most satisfying and unique lunch. Probably, the closest experience we have to this type of dish is the "shabu, shabu" in Asian restaurants, where hot broth and uncooked ingredients are brought to the table to be cooked by the patron.

There is a more popular version of the story where the husband is a scholar studying for the Imperial Examinations. He has isolated himself on an island in a lake so as not to be disturbed. His wife has to cross a long wooden bridge in order to bring him his lunch. It is always cold when she arrives. She knows he will think more clearly and can study better if he has a hot meal. She tries and fails until the same thing happens as in the above version and the oil sealing the broth keeps it hot. Needless to say, her husband passes his exams. I believe this version was also mentioned to me by Yan Lixian, national guide, as well as by the waitress whom I asked to tell me about this dish. I also heard a brief version of the scholar variant from our local Kunming guide when she asked her about the legend. (Heineman)

Storytelling Tips

As the wife is preparing the delicacies, I use chopping motions in cutting the vegetables and hold up the "paper thin" slices of meat, looking through them to see light. I flick my wrists back and forth as I swirl each ingredient into the soup and every time I say "Swish." The teller can invite the audience to "cook" the ingredients by picking them up with our chopsticks and saying "Swish, swish" out loud. It is possible to ask the audience what ingredients they might like to add, especially if there are children present. (Heineman)

A Storied Past
A Short History of Storytelling in China

Chinese storytelling, like storytelling of other cultures, started when humankind learned to talk. There is no record of this because storytelling is oral language, not written. How do we know this is true? Because we humans tell stories, learn through stories and communicate with stories. Every culture has stories that shaped the people as they shaped the stories.

When looking at a map of modern China, one can see the image of a rooster. The Chinese describe place orientations by imagining where a locale would be on the body of an imaginary rooster, which they imagine standing face-right, so that the breast forms the coastline of the Pacific Ocean, Sea of Japan and South China Sea and the tail meets Pakistan, etc., to the viewer's left. Our storytelling delegation traveled from Beijing in the rooster's neck to Guiyang and Guizhou Province in the rooster's belly and then back to Shaghai located in the rooster's chest. (See page 108)

"If we raise 3,000 men and call upon them to attack the Gongfang, we will receive abundant assistance." This is one of the divinations written on an Oracle Bone during the Shang Dynasty (1700-1027 BCE). The Oracle Bones were clavicles of oxen or turtle shells on which seers, sometimes the king, carved the question and the answer they received by reading the cracks in the bones or shells during special rituals which involved cutting a groove in the bone and then applying an extremely hot point to it in order to crack the bone. These inscriptions, known as Gia Gu Wen and believed to be the earliest form of Chinese writing, were first unearthed at Anyang in Henen Province during the late 1800's. (Hessler) Although they do not tell long stories or even folktales, these Oracle Bones are significant because they tell the stories of the Shang Dynasty's wars, agriculture, and history. There was a mythical element to the daily lives of the populace during the Shang Dynasty. Oracle Bones revealed the mysticism of ancient China and the practice of writing about important events carried on into later dynasties. (Hough)

Ancestor worship was a daily ritual for the people living during the Shang Dynasty. They believed their ancestors controlled their lives and required constant offerings of prayer and food. Oracle Bones also trace the complicated sacrifices to a wide range of natural, supernatural and spiritual phenomena through various ceremonies. Ceremonial vessels of the nobility were cast from bronze, which was in use in China over four thousand years ago. Oracle Bones and bronze ceremonial vessels are the only record of the Shang and Zhou Dynasties; all other recorded information was not able to stand the ruinous villain, Time. ("National Palace Museum")

Bronze cooking vessels produced during the Zhou Dynasty (1027-771 BCE) are called dings. Many of these three-legged vessels have Chinese characters called Jin Wen inscribed upon them. The earlier such inscriptions seem to be the names of the owners, the dates they were cast, and the uses for the vessels. Later the inscriptions told tales and legends of the time. Wars, treaties, agriculture and history are recorded on recovered dings. Also customary was the casting of inscriptions on bronze ritual vessels to record some recognition of meritorious achievement, bestowal of imperial favor, appointment to office, settlement of a contract, proclamation of a new statute, or taking of an oath. The most famous is the Mao Gong Ding which tells the legend of how Xuan, the Emperor of the late Western Zhou Dynasty, admonished, commended and awarded his relative Mao Gong Ying. The Emperor, realizing the instability of his government, asked Mao

Gong to correct the situation. When he accepted horses, chariots, weapons and ceremonial articles as well as special powers, Mao Gong had the ding cast as a record of his good fortune. (Yang) (Hough) ("Cultural China") ("National Palace Museum")

The Da Ke Zhou Ding tells the story of Zhou Wang who owned much land and had many slaves. This ding, unearthed in Shaanxi Fufeng Famen during the Qing Dynasty, describes Zhou's life and tells about the achievements of his ancestors. It is important to the study of the Western Zhou economic system and culture. ("ShanghaiMuseum.net") Legends have arisen from the inscriptions found on the dings.

During the Warring States Period (475-221 BCE) stories in the form of fables were, according to Professor Yang Lihui of the Beijing Normal University, "used for suggesting, persuading and debating." Examples of these fables are The Snipe and the Mussel, Fox Assumes Tiger's Authority, and A Blessing or a Curse. These stories along with historical anecdotes and strategies were written down in the 33 scrolls known as Zhan Guo Ce (Strategies of the Warring States). Rather than a true history of the time, it is actually a work of ancient Chinese literature. The fables come from all seven of the Warring States of that restless era of Chinese history. At a time when culture grew, greed abounded among the rulers of the Warring States so that the only end to war was for one state to conquer all the others and unite China under one ruler. The state of Qin succeeded in doing just that in 221 BCE. The scrolls were written during the Han Dynasty long after the stories were told orally. The stories that have stood the test of time are still being told today. (Huang) Like most fables, they teach valuable lessons.

The Han Dynasty (206 BCE – 220 CE) revived artistic, literary and intellectual endeavors that had been repressed by the Qin Dynasty (221-207 BCE) and saw them thrive. Thus The

Han Dynasty earned the title, The Golden Age of Performance Arts. A memorable story from the Han Dynasty is Seeking Her Husband at the Great Wall or, as it is called in this anthology, Tears that Crumbled the Great Wall. It is set during the repressive Qin Dynasty. (China Folklore Society) Stories told during the Han Dynasty were longer with more details than those of earlier times, enriching the experience for tellers and listeners. The lessons found in the stories of earlier times are not gone; they are just wrapped in extra layers.

The original ancient terra cotta Storytelling Figurine of Mount Tian Hui, found during 1957 in a burial tomb, was made during the Eastern Han Dynasty (25-220 CE), the Golden Age of the Arts, and today is in the collection of national treasures at the National Museum in Beijing. Originally, the figure was part of a group meant to provide entertainment in the afterlife. Its name comes from the locale where it was unearthed. (Harris) Later two other fascinating telling and singing statues were found along with twenty-eight statuettes that seemed to represent servants, dancers and jokesters. All symbolize types of telling and singing entertainers. The two larger statues "seem to exhibit the enchanted smile of someone carried away by his own story." They have given rise to the impetus of the study of storytelling and other early entertainment arts in China. (Børdahl) One figurine has become the face of shuoshu (storytelling). He has an animated face and a drum under one arm with a drum stick in the other hand. The stories he represents include historical anecdotes, marvels, lawsuits, martial arts legends, folktales and romance. (Yang)

The Tang Dynasty (618-907 CE) saw another renaissance of literature and art. Confucian intellectuals were selected through civil service exams as a means of drawing the best talents into the government. These scholar-officials had no autonomous territorial or functional power base, but acquired local status in their communities and families because of their ties to the imperial court. They often functioned as intermediaries between the grass-roots level and the government. Many younger sons aspired to become scholar officials, as this would ensure a life of relative prosperity while their eldest brother received the family inheritance. The story Tuiqiao is about the scholar-officials and is set during the Tang Period.

The actual telling of stories during the Tang Dynasty produced written texts based on the oral storytelling. These texts are known as bian wen or transformation texts. Storytelling during this era was known as shuohua meaning talking words instead of the more professional term shuoshu, talking books, which came into use later. (Børdahl)

Storytelling became a major source of entertainment during the Song Dynasty (960-1279 CE). Depending on the venue either shuoshu, speaking books or shouhua, speaking words, was performed in teahouses, temple fairs and story booths. This was the beginning of a more professional type of storytelling which continued until the Great Proletarian Cultural Revolution, especially in the Yangzhou region about 150 miles from Shanghai where pinghua, a long prose style of telling serialized stories, was performed in changuan, teahouses. (Fairlee)

Two famous storytellers who tell "teahouse stories" are Shan Tianfang and Liu Lanfeng. Shan Tianfeng who was born in 1935 is a man whose family had a tradition of being professional storytellers. He watched his family members perform, wrote down the stories and remembered them. He was taught by other masters outside his family and began his own telling at the age of 24. His specialty is The Romance of the Three Kingdoms. Liu Lanfeng, a woman born in 1944, received special training. Her mother was well-known locally for singing and chanting. She received training from master storytellers and specializes in historical stories which she tells in half hour sections since they are epic in length. (Yang)

Most of the stories performed in teahouses were long and serialized so that the clientele needed to return each day in order to hear the whole story. Both stories I found are very long. One "is a vernacular, humorous, lowbrow story of a beggar" called Pi Wu Lazi. The story is entitled Qing Feng Zha and takes forty hours to tell. It is told today only by Yang Mingkin, a ninth generation teller. (Fairlee) The other story tells of the overthrow of the Shang Dynasty. (Chew) These stories, when written, can be several hundred pages long. For this reason, none are included in this anthology.

Outside the city of Guiyang in Guizhou Province lies Qingyan Ancient Village. This village of 7000 was built as a fortification during the Ming Dynasty (1368-1644 CE). Professor Zhang Xiaosong from Guizhou Normal University led our delegation through the narrow streets of the village where we tasted spicy meats and mentally marked shops to which we wanted to return. We met one of the most famous elderly men of the village whose ancestors were from the same family as Premier Zhou Enlai.

At a teahouse in the heart of the village, Professor Zhang enchanted us with stories from the Miao people, who have a 7000 year history told through embroidery and batik because they were always moving from place to place to escape persecution. The Butterfly Mother is a very important creation symbol in the Miao culture. She came from the Holy Feng Tree (Maple Tree). She laid twelve eggs and with the help of the Magpie, Jiang Yang, who is the ancestor of the Miao People, they were born from these twelve eggs. And so the Butterfly Mother gave birth to the Miao People, thus, the importance of butterflies, magpies and the maple tree in this mountainous region located in the belly of the rooster. Outside of China the Miao are known as Hmong.

After our meeting at the teahouse, we wandered the narrow

streets again in search of stories and goods to purchase. Shortly after entering the village we passed through a triple archway which was erected as a monument to the Mother of Scholars. As we walked through the streets we were led to the Hall of Scholars where, during the mid to late 1800's, the most famous of scholars from the area lived with their mother. She was a widowed mother who raised her four sons to become brilliant scholars despite hardships. Because all four sons had fire as a symbol of their names, their mother had two special wells dug at the family home to subdue their fiery natures. To honor her for doing such a wonderful job raising her sons she was given permission by the Emperor to sleep in a three-chambered bed. These beds were usually only found in the Palaces where the Empress lived. At the entrance to the house gardens there is a hallway where bas relief sculptures of the four young men and their mother have been placed along with their stories.

In another part of the village we stopped in front of a Daoist Temple which had eight portraits in bas relief. These sculptures portrayed the eight immortals or ba xian representing male, female, the old, the young, the rich, the noble, the poor, and the humble Chinese; at the top, above all the rest, was a ninth figure. This sculpture represented the holy person of money or the god of making money correctly because the temple had been erected by a businessman who had immigrated to the area.

During the early part of the Ming Dynasty (1368-1644 CE) twenty-four military stations were set up in Guizhou Province by the peasant emperor Zhu Yuanzhang in order to put down the rebellions in the area. These rebellions were led by the Miao and Yao ethnic minorities. Soldiers from the central plains area around Nanjing were sent to subdue the rebellions. Spouses, families and entrepreneurs followed, bringing with them cartloads of necessities and supplies for daily life. The people who inhabited the stations were called tun pu ren or station people, but they called themselves "Nanjing people" to show they were proud of their origins. Most were soldiers first, but their families required sustenance, so many also became farmers, others because shopkeepers and tradespeople. Enterprising people, they built homes using stones gathered from the fields. Many families never returned to their former homes in Nanjing.

In order to entertain themselves and their families during their leisure time, these soldier-farmers pulled from their nuo culture of the plains and developed Dixi or Ground Opera. Because they were soldiers who fought battles and were considered heroic, the operas were mainly about battles, but also embraced elements of the traditional nuo drama which included large, elaborate, stylized wooden masks. The actors were the soldier-farmers and other men from the communities that arose around the military camps. The sizeable wooden masks actually sat above their heads while their faces were covered with black gauze, giving the actors added stature. (Xiao)

Performances for the villagers were given during the Spring Festival, Chun Jie, which is the first fifteen days of the lunar new year, and following the mid-July Harvest. These are the times of the year when there is the most leisure time for farmers. Then and now the performances may last up to twelve days and depict "historical battle stories, such as Wars between Chu and Han, the Romance of the Three Kingdoms, the History of the Sui and Tang Dynasties, and Generals of the Yang Family" emphasizing the aspects of bravery and loyalty. (Xiao)

The masks themselves are carved from wood and use symbolic colors and facial expressions to represent various characters. Faces were painted red to symbolize loyalty, black for fierceness, green meant a calm person, blue for chivalry, and white for courage. Eyebrows and beards or lack of beards also had specialized meaning. Old characters had white beards and slanted eyebrows (\ /). Young characters had the same eyebrows, but either had no beard or a black beard. Female characters, or course, had no beard and their eyebrows were feminized (˘ ˘). Representing martial arts the mask had a black beard and very bushy eyebrows. Costumes were simple and brightly colored consisting of a bright blue or black shirt and a long colorful skirt; shoes were black and soft for ease in doing the choreographed steps. Weapons were also made from wood. (Lao)

The actual stories portrayed in Dixi Opera had been told for years, but were now being acted out for the entertainment of large groups. Music was provided only by a large drum and a gong. Performances were outdoors usually in a large field with many of the spectators sitting on the low hillsides in order to obtain a better view. (Xiao) Short performances, such as the one we were privileged to witness, are now part of the tourist trade.

Storytelling in China enjoyed a renaissance beginning in the mid 1980's. In some circles this is known as the Golden Age of Storytelling. Wujiagou Village became a Story Village in 1986. In the valley of the Wudang Mountains, southwest of Beijing, lay a "living fossil of ancient culture." Since there had been little communication with the world outside the village borders many primitive legends and folktales were found here. During the 1980's "over a thousand folklores [tales] and thousands of folk songs" were discovered earning the village the name "A Village of Folklores." ("Confucius Institute Online") The 1990's brought fame, tourism and loss. Fame because some of the storytellers were thrust into the national spotlight; tourism, when groups were led to the village to listen to the stories requiring the building of better roads, hotels and other tourist necessities; loss because the way of life in the village began to change with the influx of trade and money brought by the tourists. (Yang)

1990 saw the first storytelling contest which was attended not only by storytellers but also by the media. Luo Chengshuang, one of the ten greatest storytellers in China, won first prize at this contest. He was an orphan raised by his grandmother who told him stories. During the 1950's and 1960's he learned and spread stories throughout his region. During the Great Proletarian Cultural Revolution (1966-1976) he was censored. He knows over 400 stories and 600 folksongs which he shares with listeners. Li Xiaocui, a youthful storyteller, told a story at the first storytelling contest when he was only four years old. He now takes his stories from books, TV, his own experiences, and ghost stories, which are the equivalent of our urban legends, from the campus where he attends school. (Yang)

In 2002, Eth-Noh-Tec, a storytelling troupe founded by Nancy Wang and Robert Kikuchi-Yngojo, journeyed to Gengcun Village for the first time to meet and share stories with Gengcun storytellers. The village, which has a storytelling tradition of over 600 years, is located in Hebei Province south of Beijing and northwest of Nanjing. It is home to 1200 agrarian residents. Many of the storytellers are high level tellers who know 300-500 stories. Gengcun, like Wujiagou was "discovered" in the mid 1980's to be a national treasure because "one out of ten people in this tiny village is a storyteller." (Wang) Here Nancy, Robert and their fellow travelers met Mr. Jin Jing Xian whom they compared to the American teller Ray Hicks.

Nancy writes: "With 24 Americans and one Canadian, Eth-Noh-Tec's entourage of storytellers and story lovers was greeted with female dancers in red costumes clanging bronze cymbals, while men in red costumes rhythmically beat red drums on the backs of trucks. Children lined the streets with paper flowers waving and a large banner framed with large balloons welcomed our Nu Wa delegation as our bus drove up on their dirt road to the center of their small village. As we disembarked, we were surrounded by villagers smiling and with babies to be held and photographed. We were immediately ushered into their Story Hall where we were officially welcomed by their Mayor, the Cultural Council in the neighboring city and a few Communist leaders. Of course their Master Tellers sat around the table as we shared Chinese pears. For the next three days we divided into groups and every morning and afternoon we sat in the one-room homes of the tellers and shared stories. On the final day, we created a festival of story, song and dance. We left each other in tears, for we had found that our hearts were now part of this village and the storytellers were our friends." (Wang)

Nancy and Robert have led four more tours to Gengcun and another is being planned for May, 2013. During their tour in 2010 they discussed with their hosts the need to preserve the tradition of storytelling since many young people are leaving the village for better paying jobs and some of the young families are now taking their children with them, who would otherwise be cared for by grandparents. The concern is the breakdown of the storytelling tradition which passes stories from generation to generation through telling and listening. But "when asked about it in [the] village, they said it was not a problem - that wherever their sons and daughters went, they would be telling stories and learning others." However, Eth-Noh-Tec is concerned and they are working with the villagers to create a way to keep their young adults in the village with their children by way of a story tourist business. (Wang)

During the Golden Age stories were collected from all over the remote areas of China and published in anthologies. Professor Yang Lihui compiled The Handbook of Chinese Mythology. The China Folklore Society's collections of stories come from all over China, but mostly the rural areas where 70-80% of the people lived at the time the collections were made. These people were mainly involved in an agrarian way of life where storytelling is an integral part of life. For ten years (1985-1995), the folklorists collected 25,000 story volumes from three southern counties alone. Many other volumes were collected from other rural areas. Provincial volumes then culled the stories collected by the counties. National volumes of folklore and folktales are harvested from the provincial volumes. "Storytellers are like parents providing food to folklorists doing research." (Liu)

With all these stories, the China Folklore Society's research involves both vertical and horizontal research techniques. Vertically they are trying to discover the historicity of stories, how and why they change over time. Whereas horizontal research involves the various versions of the same or similar stories told in different regions, such as Weaving Fair Lady and Water Buffalo Boy, which has multiple versions in just one province as well as varying from region to region. The folklorists do not make judgment calls on the value of a story or change anything about the teller's rendition of the story, but record it as told. Even some of the tellers are subjects of intensive research. If an excellent teller who can tell a thousand stories is discovered, that person then comes under intense scrutiny, for the researchers wonder how one person can know that many stories. (Kang)

Dr. Yue Tao, presently (2011) the general secretary of the China Folklore Society, folklorist, and professor at a northern State University, wrote a textbook which is divided seasonally. This book is of great help to teachers and librarians in their work of passing stories on to children. Just as educators in America use seasonally based activities, so do the Chinese educators. There is also a great deal of exchange going on between the China Folklore Society and the American Folklore Society, whose focus is "Keeping Folklorists Connected."

Stories Press, a publishing company located in Shanghai, has also published a multi volume set of folktales. These tales were gathered by folklorists working on the county or local level with the elders of the community. The folklore and folktales were then fed into regional organizations which looked at the story motifs and patterns. Research was done to find variations of the same tale from different regions, as well as changes in the story as it grew from generation to generation. Stories Press now pulls from the local folklore that was gathered, the regional research and on the national level from the China Folklore Society in order to bring new and different stories to their readers. Stories Press and the China Folklore Society have a working relationship with each other. (Hé) Mr. Hé Chéngwěi, chief editor of Stories Press, is also the president of the World Folklore Society and a Storytellers Group. He does storytelling training for those interested in becoming more adept at telling stories.

In July, 1963, Stories Press published their first story magazine. The magazine is now published every two weeks and many Chinese say, "I grew up reading Stories Press Magazine." This biweekly publication is written for the common person with a fourth or fifth grade education. The language is easy to read, and the stories and jokes are easily retold. Stories Press feels their goal is to bring storytelling back to the masses. Stories which are included in Stories Press Magazine must have value for the readers' lives. Those who gather the stories for the magazine look for stories which impart a significant lesson. Most of the stories are traditional but reflect on modern life. Also included are folktales and classic foreign stories. All the stories follow basic story form so they are easy to read, tell and pass on to others. The philosophy behind Stories Press is that reading stories helps people gain knowledge that impacts their lives. In 1996 the Figurine of Mount Tian Hui was chosen as their mascot and appears in the upper right hand corner on the cover of each issue. (Hé)

In the collecting of stories, elders are willing for their stories to be published as a way of preserving their cultural heritage. Because China is a collective society, the concept of individual copyright is unclear to the majority of Chinese people, especially in the rural areas where most of the stories are collected. The Chinese government plays a significant role in the preservation of Chinese folklore and folktales, both in the collection and distribution of tales. Storytelling is believed to be a true art form separate from operas (plays), movies, poems, essays and novels. Storytelling falls under the jurisdiction of the Minister of Culture. (Féng)

According to Mr. Féng Jié, the vice president of Stories Press, storytelling led to poetry which evolved into novels. Most of the novels from the Ming and Qing dynasties were based on stories told by storytellers. The novels started out being very simply written forms of stories people had heard. Gradually they became more artistic in flavor. The art of oral telling has been preserved for centuries. He believes storytelling is for everyone, which is the driving philosophy behind Stories Press. Stories Press publishes stories for everyone to retell in their own way. The magazine is a catalyst for people to find and tell stories with their families and friends. Each issue includes many shorter stories, humorous stories, jokes, new legends, stories about common issues up to four thousand words, and a novel of eight to ten thousand words. Illustrations are mainly black and white drawings since the pages are a newsprint quality, but the pictures on the website, http://www.storychina.cn/, are in brilliant color as is the magazine cover. The website includes teaser stories, pictures and audio clips. It is written entirely in Chinese. (Féng)

The issue of compensation for storytelling and the stories told is genuine—as it is elsewhere in the world. Common storytellers in the villages and other communities receive no compensation for their telling. Professional storytellers still receive compensation, but they are receiving less because their audiences are dwindling. Novelists and movie actors seem to be the best paid storytellers as is true in Western cultures. (Féng)

Today people listen to stories on the radio, children hear stories from their parents, and elders still pass stories on to future generations. Younger people, especially, watch stories on TV and the internet. Stories are passed on orally, visually and through print. Stories are an integral part of the education process. They provide lessons for children today as they always have in the past. Chinese and foreign tourists listen to stories told by tour guides and rickshaw drivers in the hutongs of Beijing which keeps the history of the Hutong areas alive. (Féng) Some tourists in groups such as the People to People Storytelling Delegation and Eth-noh-tec tours are privileged to hear stories from elders, folklorists and students.

Now traditional storytelling is competing with modern entertainment and, as in the rest of the world, losing ground. New uses for storytelling and ways of weaving the traditional tales into other activities are the means to keep storytelling alive and vibrant.

Professor Zhang Xiaosong from the College of International Tourism and Culture at the Guizhou Normal University wants to use storytelling to enhance the experience of tourists to her region. An anthropologist, Professor Zhang was an active NGO-organizer and director (Rural Tourism Development Center), ethnographer and one of the first two Chinese scholars to integrate tourism and anthropology in China.

According to Professor Zhang Xiaosong, "Everyone needs two things – a grain of rice to feed the body and a little song [story] to nourish the soul."

Map of China

Glossary of Pinyin Words and Terms

Anyang (安阳 ān yang) Northern most city in Henan Province

Bian wen (变文 biàn wén) Written texts based on oral stories

Chang'an (长安 cháng ān) Now known as Xian, Chang'an was the capital city during the Tang Dynasty.

Cha guan (茶馆 chá guǎn) Teahouses in the Yangzhou region where pinghua was practiced Chengdu (成都 chéng dū) Provincial capital of Sichuan Province

Chu (楚 chǔ) An independent state located in the middle of China during the Warring States Period (475-221 BCE)

Da Ke Zhou Ding (大克周鼎 dà kè zhōu dǐng) Ding belonging to Zhou Wang.

Ding (鼎 dǐng) Three-legged bronze vessel, used for cooking and ceremonies

Dixi Opera (地戏 dì xì) Literally Ground Opera, opera performed in open fields instead of theatres

Emei Mountains (峨眉山 é méi shān) Rugged, jagged peaks surrounded by mist and clouds and deep gullies mark this range in Sichuan Province.

Fa Hai (法海 fǎ hǎi) Monk who imprisoned Lady White

Fan Xiliang (范喜良 fàn xǐ liáng) The husband of Meng Jiang in the story of Tears that Crumbled the Great Wall

Feng (枫 fēng) Maple Tree

feng shui (风水 fēng shuǐ) The balance of energies within a given space, literally wind water, also associated with meaning of good health and therefore good fortune.

Mr. Feng Jie (冯杰 féng jié) Vice president of Stories Press in Shanghai

Gansu Province (甘肃省 gānsù shěng) Province located in the mountainous region of northwestern China

Gengcun Viallge (耿村 gěng cūn) Designated storytelling village located south of Beijing

Guizhou Province (贵州省 guì zhōu shěng) Province located in the fertile mountains of southwestern China

Guo Qiao Mi Xian (过桥米线 guò qiáo mǐ xiàn) Across the Bridge Rice Noodles

Han Dynasty (汉代 hàn dài) Western – 206 BCE-9 CE; Eastern – 25-220 CE

Han Fei Tzu (韩非子 hán fēi zǐ) Prince of the House of Han

Han Yu (韩愈 hán yú) Poet scholar and philosopher who was

an official in the city of Chang'an

Hangzhou City (杭州城 háng zhōu chéng) Capital of Zhejiang Province; located south of Shanghai

Mr. He Chengwei (何承伟 hé chéng wěi) President of Stories Press in Shanghai

Hebei Province　　　　(河北省 hé běi shěng) Province where Beijing is located

Henan Province (河南省 hé nán shěng) Province located middle eastern interior of China, south of Hebei Province.

Mr. Huang Kangle (黄康乐 huáng kāng lè) Our guide and translator in Guizhou Province and my personal contact in China who has helped with the authentication of these stories.

Jia Dao (贾岛 jiǎ dǎo) Poet scholar who wished to become an official by passing the Imperial Examination

Jia Gu Wen (甲骨文 jiǎ gǔ wén) Earliest form of Chinese writing inscribed on the Oracle Bones.

Jiang Yi (江乙 jiāng yǐ) The minister who told Xuanwang a story about a Tiger and a Fox when the king thought the northern states were afraid of his general, not himself.

Jiayu Pass (嘉峪关 jiā yù guān) Western end of the Great Wall located in Gansu Province

Mr. Jin Jing Xian (晋景祥 jìn jǐng xiáng) Elder and

storyteller from Gengcun Village

Jin Wen (金文 jīn wén) Characters inscribed on the inside of dings

Jin Xian Qiao (酒仙桥 jiǔ xiān qiáo) A community center in Beijing for retired electrical workers and their families.

Jiang Yang (姜央 jiāng yāng) Magpie

Ju Yong Guan Pass (居庸关 jū yōng guān) a portion of the Great Wall located outside Beijing

Dr. Kang Li (康丽 kāng lì) She is a member of the Chinese Folklore Society and author of books on the folklore of women

Kunming City (昆明 kūn míng) Located in southwestern Yunnan Province west of Guizhou Province.

Làn yú chōng shù (滥竽充数 làn yú chōng shù) Translation – To fill a position without having the necessary qualifications.

Li (里 lǐ) Unit of measurement usually translated as mile.

Mr. Li Kuo (李阔 lǐ kuò) Teaches Mandarin through the Chinese Guest Teacher Program of College Board Chinese Initiative and provided invaluable help with the pinyin glossary.

Li Xiaocui (李小翠 lǐ xiǎo cuì) Youthful storyteller

Liang Shanbo (梁山伯 liáng shān bó) Hero in the story

Butterfly Lovers

Liaoning Province (辽宁省 liáoníngshěng) Province located in northeastern China

Lingzhi (灵芝 língzhī) Medicinal herb known as glossy ganoderma

Liu Kuili (刘魁立 liúkuílì) 2008 President of the China Folklore Society

Liu Lanfang (刘兰芳 liúlánfāng) Famous Teahouse Storyteller

Luo Chengshuang (罗成双 luóchéngshuāng) One of China's ten greatest storytellers

Mao Gong Ding (毛公鼎 máogōngdǐng) Ding belonging to Mao Gong Yin

Mao Gong Yin (毛公暗 máogōngyīn) Relative of Emperor Xuan of the late Zhou Dynasty

Meng Jiang (孟姜女 mèngjiāngnǚ) Heroine of the story Tears that Crumbled the Great Wall. A temple was built to honor her on Fenghuangshan Mountain in Hebei Province.

Prince Min (潘王 mǐnwáng) Son of King Xuan of Qi

Mount Tian Hui (天会山 tiānhuìshān) Terra Cotta figure unearthed in a tomb on a cliff of Tianhui Mountain in Chengdu City, Sichuan Province.

Nanguo (南郭 n á n gu ō) The man who pretended he could play the y ú .

Nian (年 ni á n) Monster that attacked villages at the end of each year, now means New Year

Niu Lang (牛郎 ni ú l á ng) Water Buffalo Boy; now a star that is named for him

Pi Wu Lazi (皮五辣子 p í w ǔ l à z ǐ) The beggar in the serialized teahouse story Qing Feng Zha

Pinghua (平话 p í ng hu à) Storytelling, serialized lengthy stories

Qi (齐 q í) One of the smaller States of the Warring States Period, it lies just north of Chu which is located in the middle of modern China

Qi (气 q ì) The life force that all living things possess

Qi Xi (七夕 q ī x ī) A day for lovers; also known as the Chinese Valentine's Day

qian li ma (千里马 qi ā n l ǐ m ǎ) Translation – a thousand li horse

Qian li song e mao; li qing, qing-yi zhong (千里送鹅毛 qi ā n l ǐ s ò ng é m á o 礼轻情意重 l ǐ q ī ng q í ng y ì zh ò ng) The gift is very light, but the passion is huge.

Qin Dynasty (清代 q í ng d à i) 221-207 BCE, a repressive

dynasty that also united the Warring States into one country.

Qin Shi Huangdi (秦始皇帝 q í n sh ǐ hu á ng d ì) The man who succeeded in uniting the Warring States named himself the first emperor of Qin － Qin Shi Huangdi. Although he was cruel and repressive, he standardized many of the systems needed for a centralized government.

Qing Dynasty (清代 q ī ng d à i) 1644-1911 CE

Qing Feng Zha (清风闸 q ī ng f ē ng zh á) Humorous serialized teahouse story of a beggar

Sichuan Province (四川 s ì chu ā n) Province which borders Tibet on the east.

Shaanxi Fufeng Famen (陕西扶风法门 sh ǎ n x ī fú f ē ng f ǎ m é n) Famen town in Fufeng County west of Xian City in Shaanxi Province.

Shan Tianfang (单田芳 sh à n ti á n f ā ng) Famous Teahouse Storyteller

Shang Dynasty (商代 sh ā ng d à i) 1700-1027 BCE

Shou (寿 sh ò u) Longevity

Shuohua (说话 shu ō hu à) Storytelling, literally talking words

Shuoshu (说书 shu ō sh ū) Storytelling, literally talking books

Su-Zheng (素贞 s ù zh ē n) Lady White or the White Snake

Sui Dynasty (隋 su í) 581-617 CE

Tang Dynasty (唐 t á ng) 618-907 CE

Tuiqiao (推敲 tu ī qi ā o) Idiom literally meaning to push or knock; figuratively meaning to weigh one's words

Wan-Li Chang-Cheng (万里长城 w à n l ǐ ch á ng ch é ng) Literally 10,000 Li Long Wall as the Great Wall of China is known in China.

Wudang Mountains (武当山 w ǔ d ā ng sh ā n) Small mountain range located western Hebei Province

Wujiagou Village (伍家沟 w ǔ ji ā g ō u) Designated storytelling village located southwest of Beijing

Xian   (西安 x ī ā n) Once known as Chang'an, but now renowned for being the home of the Terra Cotta Warriors

Xiao Qing (小青 xi ǎ o q ī ng) The Green Snake, sister of Lady White

Xu Xian (许仙 x ǔ xi ā n) Husband of Lady White

King Xuan of Qi (齐宣王 q í xu ā n w á ng) Ruled from 342-324 BCE

Xuanwang (宣王 xu ā n w á ng) King of the State of Chu (362 BCE) during the Warring States Period
Yalu River (鸭绿江 y ā l ù ji ā ng) Eastern end of the Great Wall located in Liaoning Province

Ms Yan Lixian (闫立新 yán lì xīn) Our guide and translator on the National Storytelling Network People to People Storytelling Tour of China

Dr. Yang Lihui (杨利慧 yáng lì huì) She is the first PhD in Folklore and in 2008 the director of the China Folklore Society

Yang Mingkin (杨明坤 yáng míng kūn) Teahouse Storyteller who tells Qing Feng Zha

Yangzhou Region (扬州 yáng zhōu) A transportation hub because of its excellent location at the junction of the Yangtze, the Grand Canal and the Huaihe River, also known for its cultural heritage, the seat of professional storytelling in its heyday.

Yin Yang (阴阳 yīn yang) Opposite and complementary principles representing the feminine and masculine in Daoist philosophy

Yú (竽 yú) A melodious reed pipe made of bamboo used in Ancient China

Ye Tao (叶涛 yè tāo) 2008 Secretary-general of the China Folklore Society

Zhan Guo Ce (战国策 zhàn guó cè) Strategies of the Warring States Period – 33 scrolls containing the fables and stories of the Warring States Period
Professor Zhang Xiaosong (张晓松 zhāng xiǎo sōng) Our guide at Qingyan Ancient Town

Zhejiang Province (浙江 zhè jiāng) Province located in

southeastern China, low on the rooster's chest.

Zhi Nu (织女 zh ī n ǚ) Weaving Fair Lady; now a star named for her

Zhou Dynasty (周 zh ō u) 1027-771 BCE

Master Zhou (周 zh ō u) Ran the boarding school that both Zhu Yingtai and Liang Shanbo attended in Butterfly Lovers

Zhou Wang (周望 zh ō u w ǎ ng) Very rich man who lived during the Zhou Dynasty.

Zhao Xixu (昭奚恤 zh ā o x ī x ù) Xuanwang's general

Zhu Yingtai (祝英台 zh ù y ī ng t á i) Heroine in the story Butterfly Lovers

Zhu Yuanzhang (朱元璋 zh ū yu á n zh ā ng) Peasant Emperor of the Ming Dynasty, he was the first Ming Emperor

Bibliographic References
People

China Folklore Society. Discussion of Folklore, Folktales and the Role of Storytelling in Chinese Folklore. National Storytelling Network People to People Storytelling Delegation to China. 16 Apr 2008.

Féng Jié. "How Do Storytelling Themes Vary from East to West?" National Storytelling Network People to People Storytelling Delegation to China. 23 Apr 2008.

Harris, Sheila. "Storytelling Figurine." Message to Julie Moss Herrera. 13 Dec 2010.

Hé Chéng Wěi. "How Do Storytelling Themes Vary from East to West?" National Storytelling Network People to People Storytelling Delegation to China. 23 Apr 2008.

Huáng Kānglè. Personal Interview by delegates of the National Storytelling Network People to People Storytelling Delegation. 19-22 Apr 2008.

Huáng Kānglè. "Chinese Storytelling and Stories." Messages to Julie Moss Herrera.Summer 2009 through September 2011. Email.

Kāng Lì. Discussion of Folklore, Folktales and the Role of Storytelling in Chinese Folklore. National Storytelling Network People to People Storytelling Delegation to China. 16 Apr 2008.

Professor Lao Long Fung. "The History of Dixi Opera." National Storytelling Network People to People Storytelling Delegation to China. 22 Apr 2008.

Lǐ Kuò. Personal Interviews by Julie Moss Herrera. 21, 23, 24 Sep 2011.

Lǐ Kuò. "Pinyin Glossary." Messages to Julie Moss Herrera. September and October, 2011. Email.

Liú Kuí Lì. Discussion of Folklore, Folktales and the Role of Storytelling in Chinese Folklore. National Storytelling Network People to People Storytelling Delegation to China. 16 Apr 2008.

Yán Lixian. Personal Interviews by delegates of the National Storytelling Network People to People Storytelling Delegation. 15-25 Apr 2008.

Yáng Lì Huì. "Development of Storytelling in Chinese Culture." National Storytelling Network People to People Storytelling Delegation to China. 16 Apr 2008.

Zhāng Xiāo Sōng. Discussion of the Ethnic Minorities Located in Guizhou Province and Tour ofQingyan Ancient Town. National Storytelling Network People to People Storytelling Delegation to China. 20 Apr 2008.

Zhāng Xiāo Sōng. Personal Interiew by Julie Herrera. 20 Apr 2008.

Zhōu Xiāo Ping. Series of Personal Interviews by Julie Herrera. Winter 2009/2010.

Print

Ancient Chinese Fables. Disruptive Pub, 2007. Print

Chew, Katherine Liang. Tales of the Teahouse Retold: Investiture of the Gods. New York: Writers Club Press, 2002. Print

Chai, May-lee and Winberg Chai. China A to Z: Everything You Need to Know to Understand Chinese Customs and Culture. New York: Penguin Group, 2007. Print.

Chin, Yin-Lien C., Yetta S. Center, Yin-Lien C. Chin. Chinese Folktales: An Anthology. M. E. Sharpe, 1996. Print.

Fairlee, Cathryn. Nine Generations of The Yangzhou Pinghua Story Qing Feng Zha or Pi Wu Laiz. Master's Thesis for Sonoma State University, 2008. Unpublished Print.

Fu, Shelley. Ho Yi and Other Classic Chinese Tales. Linnet Books, 2001. Print.

Hieneman, Judith. Across the Bridge Rice Noodles. 2010. Unpublished Print.

Hessler, Peter. Oracle Bones: a Journey through Time in China. HarperCollins, 2006. Print.

Krasno, Rena and Yeng-Fong Chiang. Cloud Weavers: Ancient Chinese Legends. Pacific View Press, 2003. Print.

Li, Qinjan, and Ding, Hua. Easy Way to Learn Chinese Proverbs, New World Press, 1998. Print

Spagnoli, Cathy. Asian Tales and Tellers. Atlanta: August House, 1998. Print.

Yip, Mingmei. Chinese Children's Favorite Stories. Tuttle, 2004. Print.

Yuan, Haiwang. The Magic Lotus Lantern and other Tales from Han Chinese. Libraries Unlimited, Inc., 2006. Print.

Internet Sites

"Chinese Sayings." Transname.com: Chinese/Kanji Tattoo Design. Transname.com. 2011. Web. Oct. 2011. <http://www.transname.com/sayings.html>.

Crozier, Justin. "A Unique Experiment." China in Focus Magazine Summer 2020: n, pag. Web. Nov 2009. <http://www.sacu.org/examinations.html>.

"Going Trough History Reading China." SoundsSeeChina. Sounds See China, 2007. Web. 22 Aug. 2011. < http://www.soundseechina.com/en/culture/cul_300.shtml>.

Hough, Joshua. "Shang (c.1600-1066 B.C.) & Zhou (1066-771 B.C.) Dynasties." History of Chinese Calligraphy. 22 Jan 2010. Web. Oct 2010 < http://www.art-virtue.com/history/shang-zhou/shang-zhou.htm >.

Lau, J. "The Lost Horse." YellowBridge, 2011. Web. 29 Aug 2011.

<http://www.yellowbridge.com/literature/horse.php>.

"Leifeng Pagoda (Thundering Peak Pagoda)." Seeraa
International. Seeraa International, 2011. Web. Mar2010.
<http://www.seeraa.com/china-attractions/leifeng-pagoda.html>.

Lindy, Elaine. "The Young Head of the Household." "Stories to
Grow By" with Whootie Owl!. Whootie Owl Productions, 1998.
Web. Feb 2008.
<http://www.storiestogrowby.com/stories/young_head_family_
china.html>

Manal, Naima. "What Is Ganoderma Lucidum?" eHow Health.
eHow, 2011. Web. Mar 2011.
<http://www.ehow.com/about_4671788_what-ganoderma-
lucidum.html>.

"Mao Gong Ding." Cultural China. Cultural-china.com, 2010.
Web. Oct 2010.
<http://arts.cultural-china.com/en/30Arts4836.html>.

Michaelson, Carol. "The Thousand Li Horses." Orientations Nov.
1999: n.pag. Web. 28 Aug. 2011.
< http://publications.kaleden.com/articles/487.html>.

Knoblock, John. "Han Fei." The Classical Chinese Philosophy
Page." University of Miami, 10 Aug 1996. Web. 24 Aug 2011.
<http://www.as.miami.edu/phi/bio/buddha/hanfei.htm>.

Peterson, Erik E. "Units of Length." On-line Chinese Tools. Erik
E. Peterson, 2005. Web. May 2010.
< http://www.mandarintools.com/measures.html>.

"The Ritual Bronze Vessels of the Shang and Chou Dynasties."
National Palace Museum, 11 Nov 2010. Web. Oct 2010.
<http://www.npm.gov.tw/exhbition/cves2000/english/eves2000.
htm>.

Schrist. "Chinese Parables of the Perfect Horse." Everything2. The
Everything Development Company, 08 Feb. 2002. Web. 19 Aug.
2011.
<http://everything2.com/title/Chinese+parables+of+the+perfect+
horse>.

Schrist. "Push or Knock." Everything2. Everything2, 10 Mar
2002. Web. Feb 2010.
<http://everything2.com/title/
push+or+knock?searchy=search>.

"Shanghai Museum." ShanghaiMuseum.net. Shanghai Museum,
2008. Web. Oct 2010.
<http://www.shanghaimuseum.net/en/index.jsp>

"Snakes: the Chinese Legend of White Snake." Chinese Fortune
Calendar. Web. Jan 2009.
<http://www.chinesefortunecalendar.com/whitesnake.htm>

"Top Ten Most Popular Travel Attraction Destinations in China.
Just Travel China. JustTravelChina.com, 2011. Web. 4 Aug 2011.
< http://www.justtravelchina.com/>.

"Traditional Fetivals in China. Travel China Guide.
TravelChinaGuide.com, 2011. Web. 2 Aug 2010.
< http://www.travelchinaguide.com/essential/holidays/>

Vibeke Børdahl. "History and Milieu." Chinese Storytelling.
N.p., n.d. Web. July 2011.
<http://www.shuoshu.org/Chinese_Storytelling/History_and_
milleu/index.shtml>

Xiao, Xiao. "Chinese Ground Opera – Anshun Dixi Opera."
Interact China. Interact China, n.d. Web. 17 Aug 2011.
< http://interactchina.wordpress.com/2011/06/14/chinese-
ground-opera-anshun-dixi-drama/ >.

"yinyang." Encyclopædia Britannica. Encyclopædia Britannica
Online. Encyclopædia Britannica, 2011. Web. Mar. 2010.
<http://www.britannica.com/EBchecked/topic/653297/yinyang>.

"Zhan Guo Ce (Strategies of the Warring States)." Cultural
China. Shanghai New and Press Bureau, 2010. We. Feb 2010.
<http://history.culturalchina.com/en/174History8485.html>